I Want More
of
You Jesus

I Want More
of
You Jesus

By Daniel E. Springs

To order additional copies of this book, contact:
Xlibris Corporation
1-888-795-4274
www.Xlibris.com
Orders@Xlibris.com
81186

TABLE OF CONTENTS

DEDICATION PAGE

I dedicate this work first to the Father-Yahweh and who sent his son Yahshua-The Lord Jesus Christ who left us with the Holy Spirit who counseled me in the manuscript being our Counselor. May all glory be to God and it is written that he might be glorified and that you might receive the anointing, His name is Jesus.

To my Mother and Father who have been received by his Holy hands to His Holy Place in heaven whom the Lord used as instruments that I might have life eternal through the knowledge of His Son, who came into the world to save all from sin.

Then my family, who quietly listened and allowed me to speak in his name then interact with joy when His name is spoken, Jesus the Christ. Peace be unto you Sheila, Michael, James, Sharon, Hilda, Jimmie, Jackie, Aaron Jr. and my Auntie and family members.

If you do not know the Lord Jesus Christ or were never told about his name or the gospel, let me take a moment to introduce Him to you by the Roman Road. The Bible says first that:

While we were in our sin Christ died for us.

- Romans 5:8

For all have sinned and come short of the glory of God,

- Romans 3:23

For the wages of sin is death, but the free gift of God is eternal life in Christ Jesus our Lord.

- Romans 6:23

For the wrath of God is revealed from heaven against all ungodliness and unrighteousness of men
                                                        - Romans 1:18

Much more then, being now justified by His blood, we shall be saved from wrath thru Him.
                                                        - Romans 5:9

Even the righteousness of god which is by faith of Jesus Christ unto all and upon them that believe…
                                                        - Romans 3:22

If you confess with your mouth Jesus as Lord, and believe in your heart that God raised Him from the dead, you will be saved; for with the heart a person believes, resulting in righteousness, and with the mouth he confesses, resulting in salvation.
                                                        - Romans 10:9-10

For Whosoever will call on the name of the Lord will be saved.
                                                        - Romans 10:13

Pray like this: Father God, I have sinned and I want to repent. Please forgive me of my sins by the blood of Jesus Christ that was shed for me on the cross that I might be cleanse and made whole and new in your sight (perfectly clean and spotless). Baptize me in water and then baptize me with your Holy Spirit that I might walk in the spirit in obedience to your will for my life. And I thank you for doing this in Christ Jesus Holy name. Happy Birthday, remember this day, your name is written in the God's book of Life.

Dear Father, please bless Iris Chen for her cover design and graphic work in Christ Jesus name.

"For whoever will call on the name of the Lord will be saved."
Romans 10:13

JONAH
ESTHER
DANIEL
FASTS
&
FASTING FOR NATIONAL REPENTANCE
BOWING IN SACKCLOTH AND ASHES FOR AMERICA

SACKCLOTH,

2 Kings 19:1	FASTING HEZEKIAH
1 Chronicles 21:16	DAVID AT THE FLOOR
Esther 4:1-4	ESTHER-NATIONAL
Isaiah 58:5	FAST HE CHOSEN
Daniel 9:3-20	DANIEL-NATIONAL
Jonah 3:5-8	JONAH-NATIONAL
Nehemiah 9:1	NEHEMIAH-NATIONAL
Joel 2:12-32	ISRAEL-NATIONAL Joel 2:1-32
2 Chron 20:1-30	JUDAH-NATIONAL AND PROTECT
Matt 6:18	HOW TO FAST? (FROM WORDS OF JESUS)

God wants us to fast. Then we will find joy and peace in our lives. For God hears our prayers and listens to the desires of our hearts. It is with this dimension of self-sacrifice that He sees our desires. Jesus fasted often and in the garden gave of himself for us. Should we not do the same for Him who loved us. There are many people that would say, "this isn't the right time for endeavoring to abstain the flesh from its' comforts" but now is the time for darkness is upon the land.

What I want you to know in these pages that God (Jehovah Rapha-Yahweh) has given us these tools our human bodies to be perfected instruments for Him and only tuned finely may they make a sound that gives a perfect pitch Anna found it so Let's look at her life.

Luke 2:36-40 *And there was one Anna, a prophetess, the daughter of Phanuel, of the tribe of Aser: she was of a great age, and had lived with an husband seven years from her virginity; 37 And she [was] a widow of about fourscore and four years, which departed not from the temple, but served [God] with fastings and prayers night and day. 38 And she coming in that instant gave thanks likewise unto the Lord, and spake of him to all them that looked for redemption in Jerusalem. {Jerusalem: or, Israel} 39 And when they had performed all things according to the law of the Lord, they returned into Galilee, to their own city Nazareth. 40 And the child grew, and waxed strong in spirit, filled with wisdom: and the grace of God was upon him.*

God wanted her to be a signal that worship is the key to His heart. His name is Holy, <u>without holiness no man shall see God</u>. This is why she found grace in the sight of God and was presented with the child Jesus Christ the messiah. She gave of herself so God blessed her. She seeing His face was delighted to see her king. "I alone Am the Lord Most High!" I give life to whom I wish. Moses was on the mountain for forty days and forty nights without nourishment of a human sort but the power of Jehovah Jireh-The Great I AM sustained Him.

Exodus 34:27-29 *And the LORD said unto Moses, Write thou these words: for after the tenor of these words I have made a covenant with thee and with Israel. 28 And he was there with the LORD forty days and forty nights; <u>he did neither eat bread, nor drink water.</u> And he wrote upon the tables the words of the covenant, the ten commandments. {commandments: Heb. words} 29 And it came to pass, when Moses came down from mount Sinai with the two tables of testimony in Moses' hand, when he came down from the mount, that Moses wist not that the skin of his face shone while he talked with him.*

That is why I give grace to the hopeless and strength to the weak. Many will be blessed by the Lord as they seek my face through giving of themselves taking away pleasant desires of the flesh. You see I AM a God who cares for their strength and anoint by the Glory of the Lord to sustain mankind. This is a small thing in my sight. The body, mind soul and strength I give to mankind each day the source of which I give. "Hearken to the voice of the Lord," I give graciously to all who seek my face and listen to my words as Moses did. There is another Daniel who cried out to me:

Daniel 10:2-9 *In those days I Daniel was mourning three full weeks. 3 I ate no pleasant bread, neither came flesh nor wine in my mouth, neither did I anoint myself at all, till three whole weeks were fulfilled. 4 And in the four and twentieth day of the first month, as I was by the side of the great river, which [is] Hiddekel; 5 Then I lifted up mine eyes, and looked, and behold a certain man clothed in linen, whose loins [were] girded with fine gold of Uphaz: 6 His body also [was] like the beryl, and his face as the appearance of lightning, and his eyes as lamps of fire, and his arms and his feet like in colour to polished brass, and the voice of his words like the voice of a multitude. 7 And I Daniel alone saw the vision: for the men that were with me saw not the vision; but a great quaking fell upon them, so that they fled to hide themselves. 8 Therefore I was left alone, and saw this great vision, and there remained no strength in me: for my comeliness was turned in me into corruption, and I retained no strength. 9 Yet heard I the voice of his words: and when I heard the voice of his words, then was I in a deep sleep on my face, and my face toward the ground.*

I took his sacrifice and made him to see that which was important to me. Daniel thirsted and fasted until he saw the angel Gabriel with the message I had sent him with. When we fast there will be strongholds lifted then joy will come in the morning. His breakthrough came after his body had went through a period intense preparation before the vision came. I can't give such knowledge without a longing to be purged on the altar of fiery costliness. There are many who started the process then wore out before the "time of blessings" to be received. I sent my prophets to be a sign of this grace but they were not accepted. John the baptist was one of so.

Mark 1: 3-9 *The voice of one crying in the wilderness, Prepare ye the way of the Lord, make his paths straight. 4 John did baptize in the wilderness, and preach the baptism of repentance for the remission of sins. 5 And there went out unto him all the land of Judaea, and they of Jerusalem, and were all baptized of him in the river of Jordan, confessing their sins. 6 And John was clothed with camel's hair, and with a girdle of a skin about his loins; and he did eat locusts and wild honey; 7 And preached, saying, There cometh one mightier than I after me, the latchet of whose shoes I am not worthy to stoop down and unloose. 8 I indeed have baptized you with water: but he shall baptize you with the Holy Ghost.*

He did not eat of but the food prepared by God. He made himself holy on account of me therefore he was given the gospel of repentance to teach the nation of Israel. They saw something within him and knew I had spoken. When you preach the gospel, don't forget to fast and pray and then I will see your sacrifice and allow my angels to tell you words to say that will impact the lives of those I send to you that day. It cannot come without a sacrifice. The Lord Jesus gave of Himself twice, while he worshiped me in the garden and when the Holy Ghost led Him in the desert then He was tempted. In the garden he was more pure than at any other time.

Luke 22:40 *And when he was at the place, he said unto them, Pray that ye enter not into temptation. 41 And he was withdrawn from them about a stone's cast, and kneeled down, and prayed, 42 Saying, Father, if thou be willing, remove this cup from me: nevertheless not my will, but thine, be done. 43 And there appeared an angel unto him from heaven, strengthening him. 44 And being in an agony he prayed more earnestly: and his sweat was as it were great drops of blood falling down to the ground. 45 And when he rose up from prayer, and was come to his disciples, he found them sleeping for sorrow, 46 And said unto them, Why sleep ye? rise and pray, lest ye enter into temptation.*

I sent My Son to give evidence that petitions that arise through agony of grace will be heard when you call out to me and My Son will intercede perfecting being your High Priest. Believe on His name and your request will be heard. He is the Son of God, thy Healer of all diseases. If you will abstain from fleshly lusts then he will give you life everlasting if you believe on His name. When he spoke the enemy was astounded at His consistent ignoring the temptations that the enemy spoke to Him.

Luke 4:1-13 *And Jesus being full of the Holy Ghost returned from Jordan, and was led by the Spirit into the wilderness, 2 Being forty days tempted of the devil. And in those days he did eat nothing: and when they were ended, he afterward hungered. 3 And the devil said unto him, If thou be the Son of God, command this stone that it be made bread. 4 And Jesus answered him, saying,*

It is written, That man shall not live by bread alone, but by every word of God. 5 And the devil, taking him up into an high mountain, shewed unto him all the kingdoms of the world in a moment of time. 6 And the devil said unto him, All this power will I give thee, and the glory of them: for that is delivered unto me; and to whomsoever I will I give it. 7 If thou therefore wilt worship me, all shall be thine. 8 And Jesus answered and said unto him, Get thee behind me, Satan: for it is written, Thou shalt worship the Lord thy God, and him only shalt thou serve. 9 And he brought him to Jerusalem, and set him on a pinnacle of the temple, and said unto him, If thou be the Son of God, cast thyself down from hence: 10 For it is written, He shall give his angels charge over thee, to keep thee: 11 And in [their] hands they shall bear thee up, lest at any time thou dash thy foot against a stone. 12 And Jesus answering said unto him, It is said, Thou shalt not tempt the Lord thy God. 13 And when the devil had ended all the temptation, he departed from him for a season.

There are temptations that may come but fasting makes it evident which choices to make. Then your heart will listen to the Father. It is he who will speak to your heart and allow you to decide how to please Him. Jesus went through a lot for you and now shall you say we cannot partake of His sufferings. "Worship the Lord!" For this cause many suffer and the body of the Lord will seem powerless until we decide to allow ourselves to live according to His principles that govern His will for our lives.

Don't eat what is not good for you. In Daniel there was many foods that were presented for offerings to gods. However Daniel set in His heart not to be a worshiper of the flesh but to remain holy before the God of all graces and infinite mercies-The King of Israel-The Most High.

Daniel 1:8-21 *But Daniel purposed in his heart that he would not defile himself with the portion of the king's meat, nor with the wine which he drank: therefore he requested of the prince of the eunuchs that he might not defile himself. 9 Now God had brought Daniel into favour and tender love with the prince of the eunuchs. 10 And the prince of the eunuchs said unto Daniel, I fear my lord the king, who hath appointed your meat and your drink: for why should he see your faces worse liking than the children which [are] of your sort? then shall ye make [me] endanger my head to the king. 11 Then said Daniel to Melzar, whom the prince of the eunuchs had set over Daniel, Hananiah, Mishael, and Azariah, 12 Prove thy servants, I beseech thee, ten days; and let them give us pulse to eat, and water to drink. 13 Then let our countenances* *be looked upon before thee, and the countenance of the children that eat of the portion of the king's meat: and as thou seest, deal with thy servants. 14 So he consented to them in this matter, and proved them ten days. 15 And at the end of ten days their countenances appeared fairer and fatter in flesh than all the children which did eat the portion of the king's meat. 16 Thus Melzar took away the portion of their meat, and the wine that they should drink; and gave them pulse. 17 As for these four children, God gave them knowledge and skill in all learning and wisdom: and Daniel had understanding in all visions and dreams. 18 Now at the end of the days that the king had said he should bring them in, then the prince of the eunuchs brought them in before Nebuchadnezzar. 19 And the king communed with them; and among them all was found none like Daniel, Hananiah, Mishael, and Azariah: therefore stood they before the king. 20 And in all matters of wisdom [and] understanding, that the king enquired of them, he found them ten times better than all the magicians [and] astrologers that [were] in all his realm. 21 And Daniel continued [even] unto the first year of king Cyrus.*

This is to say, that once one sets His heart on doing the will of God, there shall be innumerable blessings when He is pleased with you. Therefore, let us please our Angel of the Lord when he speaks and gives us commandments to follow. There was nothing withheld from Daniel when he set his course to follow God wholeheartedly. We shall see more as we look at the Book of Jonah. When the people heard the prophetic message of repentance they sought to humbled themselves in getting on their knees before God.

Jonah 3:1-10 *And the word of the LORD came unto Jonah the second time, saying, 2 Arise, go unto Nineveh, that great city, and preach unto it the preaching that I bid thee. 3 So Jonah arose, and went unto Nineveh, according to the word of the LORD. Now Nineveh was an exceeding great city of three days' journey. 4 And Jonah began to enter into the city a day's journey, and he cried, and said, Yet forty days, and Nineveh shall be overthrown. 5 So the people of Nineveh believed God, and proclaimed a fast, and put on sackcloth, from the greatest of them even to the least of them. 6 For word came unto the king of Nineveh, and he arose from his throne, and he laid his robe from him, and covered [him] with sackcloth, and sat in ashes. 7 And he caused [it] to be proclaimed and published through Nineveh by the decree of the king and his nobles, saying, Let neither man nor beast, herd nor flock, taste any thing: let them not feed, nor drink water: 8 But let man and beast be covered with sackcloth, and cry mightily unto God: yea, let them turn everyone from his* *evil way, and from the violence that [is] in their hands. 9 Who can tell [if] God will turn and repent, and turn away from his fierce anger, that we perish not? 10 And God saw their works, that they turned from their evil way; and God repented of the evil, that he had said that he would do unto them; and he did [it] not.*

This is why there is a dirth in the land, no one repents and does My will sayeth the Lord. If America would fall on its' knees and cry saying "Lord forgive us?" Then will I hear from heaven and as I promised:

2 Chronicles 7:12-15 *And the LORD appeared to Solomon by night, and said unto him, I have heard thy prayer, and have chosen this place to myself for an house of sacrifice. 13 If I shut up heaven that there be no rain, or if I command the locusts to devour the land, or if I send pestilence among my people; 14 If my people, which are called by my name, shall humble themselves, and pray, and seek my face, and turn from their wicked ways; then will I hear from heaven, and will forgive their sin, and will heal their land. 15 Now mine eyes shall be open, and mine ears attent unto the prayer [that is made] in this place*

If you seek my face then I will come to your rescue. However, if you chase after foreign idols and worship the false gods in your midst then I shall not help you when calamity befalls you as it saids in the rest of that chapter.

2 Chronicles 7:17 *And as for thee, if thou wilt walk before me, as David thy father walked, and do according to all that I have commanded thee, and shalt observe my statutes and my judgments; 18 Then will I stablish the throne of thy kingdom, according as I have covenanted with David thy father, saying, There shall not fail thee a man [to be] ruler in Israel. 19 But if ye turn away, and forsake my statutes and my commandments, which I have set before you, and shall go and serve other gods, and worship them; 20 Then will I pluck them up by the roots out of my land which I have given them; and this house, which I have sanctified for my name, will I cast out of my sight, and will make it [to be] a proverb and a byword among all nations. 21 And this house, which is high, shall be an astonishment to every one that passeth by it; so that he shall say, Why hath the LORD done thus unto this land, and unto this house? 22 And it shall be answered, Because they forsook the LORD God of their fathers, which brought them forth out of the land of Egypt, and laid hold on other gods, and worshipped them, and served them: therefore hath he brought all this evil upon them.*

Purity begins from a heart that is lifted up to the Lord in praise and worship. They may have ulterior motives but He hears the cry of the heart such as when Esther' prayer rose up to Heaven before His holy throne.

<u>Esther 4:10-5:2</u> *Again Esther spake unto Hatach, and gave him commandment unto Mordecai; 11 All the king's servants, and the people of the king's provinces, do know, that whosoever, whether man or woman, shall come unto the king into the inner court, who is not called, [there is] one law of his to put [him] to death, except such to whom the king shall hold out the golden sceptre, that he may live: but I have not been called to come in unto the king these thirty days. 12 And they told to Mordecai Esther's words. 13 Then Mordecai commanded to answer Esther, Think not with thyself that thou shalt escape in the king's house, more than all the Jews. 14 For if thou altogether holdest thy peace at this time, [then] shall there enlargement and deliverance arise to the Jews from another place; but thou and thy father's house shall be destroyed: and who knoweth whether thou art come to the kingdom for [such] a time as this? 15 Then Esther bade [them] return Mordecai [this answer], 16 <u>Go, gather together all the Jews that are present in Shushan, and fast ye for me, and neither eat nor drink three days, night or day: I also and my maidens will fast likewise; and so will I go in unto the king, which [is] not according to the law: and if I perish, I perish.</u> 17 So Mordecai went his way, and did according to all that Esther had commanded him. 5:1 Now it came to pass on the third day, that Esther put on [her] royal [apparel], and stood in the inner court of the king's house, over against the king's house: and the king sat upon his royal throne in the royal house, over against the gate of the house. 2 And it was so, when the king saw Esther the queen standing in the court, [that] she obtained favour in his sight: and the king held out to Esther the golden sceptre that [was] in his hand. So Esther drew near, and touched the top of the sceptre.*

Send your fire on the altar of our hearts dear Lord. That is what I want to hear. So if you give me your requests without giving me a sacrifice how shall I let the fire come down. For didn't Esther give of herself and the people with her their sacrifice that I might flood the nation with peace. That the Nation of Israel would be saved. That is what I will do to America if my people who are called by my name will give the acceptable offering of fasting and worship and rending their hearts as in Isaiah.

Isaiah 58:1-13 *Cry aloud, spare not, lift up thy voice like a trumpet, and shew my people their transgression, and the house of Jacob their sins. 2 Yet they seek* *me daily, and delight to know my ways, as a nation that did righteousness, and forsook not the ordinance of their God: they ask of me the ordinances of justice; they take delight in approaching to God. 3 <u>Wherefore have we fasted, [say they], and thou seest not? [wherefore] have we afflicted our soul, and thou takest no knowledge? Behold, in the day of your fast ye find pleasure, and exact all your labours. 4 Behold, ye fast for strife and debate, and to smite with the fist of wickedness: ye shall not fast as [ye do this] day, to make your voice to be heard on high. 5 Is it such a fast that I have chosen? a day for a man to afflict his soul? [is it] to bow down his head as a bulrush, and to spread sackcloth and ashes [under him]? wilt thou call this a fast, and an acceptable day to the LORD? 6</u>*

[Is] not this the fast that I have chosen? to loose the bands of wickedness, to undo the heavy burdens, and to let the oppressed go free, and that ye break every yoke? 7 [Is it] not to deal thy bread to the hungry, and that thou bring the poor that are cast out to thy house? when thou seest the naked, that thou cover him; and that thou hide not thyself from thine own flesh? 8 Then shall thy light break forth as the morning, and thine health shall spring forth speedily: and thy righteousness shall go before thee; the glory of the LORD shall be thy rereward. *9 Then shalt thou call, and the LORD shall answer; thou shalt cry, and he shall say, Here I [am]. If thou take away from the midst of thee the yoke, the putting forth of the finger, and speaking vanity; 10 And [if] thou draw out thy soul to the hungry, and satisfy the afflicted soul; then shall thy light rise in obscurity, and thy darkness [be] as the noonday: 11 And the LORD shall guide thee continually, and satisfy thy soul in drought, and make fat thy bones: and thou shalt be like a watered garden, and like a spring of water, whose waters fail not. 12 And [they that shall be] of thee shall build the old waste places: thou shalt raise up the foundations of many generations; and thou shalt be called, The repairer of the breach, The restorer of paths to dwell in.*

He calls us to set free the oppressed. To break the bonds of the enemy's kingdom.

PSALMS OF JESUS

THEY LOOK THE OTHER WAY WHEN I CALL OUT TO THEM JANUARY 19, 2010

JUDE 1:2 Mercy, grace truth be multiplied. Many need the grace of God but don't know how to get it. They worship me in the wrong way, science tells them evolution. They take prayer out of school replace with sheets on human definitions of the male and female sexual parts. They look in the mirror and see woman standing in man's clothes. They don't know how to say I'm seriously in need of you Father in heaven and your Savior the Lord Jesus Christ. Got it all backwards, they think, "I can do" as they take on but forget I Am the one, angels bow to, I Am the Master of All.

Furnishings when you call
I don't need a man o tell me what to do
When you worry
I'm thinking of you
Why my child
Are you letting the world bend you their way?
When I sacrificed and gave you
The release of joy in your soul
As you sang to me
A wonderful symphony of
When darkness filled your soul
And you needed a way out
I AM here for you.

Lord you are so gracious and merciful

20

WHEN YOU LOOK AT OTHER CHOICES AND DON'T REMEMBER ME JANUARY 19, 2010

It's a moneymaker
That's what they say
When they get your ideas
Maybe and say
I'll give you a hundred million if you'll play
The tune we want to hear
And leave the cross
That you hold dear
I can't make you see this is mine
We're very sorry, maybe another time
They'll listen when you talk of action and semen
Portly stares when you walk out and leave them
They look at you strangely
When they have lost the way
Whenever they leave the Light and Way of Truth

Jesus we need the Father's will for our lives, lead us to your throne of mercy and grace

THEY ARE LIKE ME MARCH 12, 2010

They are like fire in the sky
They sing your grace
When winter flowers come
They remember your glory
How you gave your hands and feet to the smiters
To purchase our pardon
They are like the Holy Ones that
Reside in the heavenly place
Speaking of Wisdom, the Fear of God, Holiness, Understanding, Counseling, Might, Knowledge, Isaiah 11:2
They cause me to fear and know and then I can decide about materials to give to others.
I worship thee
Those who know your name have a healthy fear of God.

You are worthy of all praise

WHEN I LOOK TO THE HEAVENS I SEE HIM
MARCH 13, 2010

Like a smooth stone
Angels encircling all around the throne
Rushing
The Master Of Israel is pleased
Like a violin you want me to play you
"So I will!"
Bless your name in Heaven
Bless you Lord
Let nothing live without breathing you
Worship you upon the throne
Ann nay kay yheeeee
Shimmering glory before the throne
The Light of God is present here
Whenever you write they will know
Now I go
It must be time
To loose angels upon the earth
Father bless loose your magnifying heavenly hosts in our midst
Touch our lives with your heart of love
Forgive our nation
Grant us grace in thy sight
Leave us not behind
Bring us to the place of His majesty's satisfaction before your face
Let us not be like the unrighteous who don't know the way and fall into
the pit
Help us our God
For your namesake help us Our God.

Bless your name Father

ARMOUR BATTLE SONG FOR THE LORD
MAY 1, 2010

Bless all the angels today
As they sing
Da Da Dah Da Da Da

Da Da Da Da Da Da
He's mighty in the clouds
And we worship him another day
Come Gabriel upon the horn
Loud trumpet blast
And Michael play the guitar
Let His praises fill the Heavens (thunderous stomping)
Oh glorify His name (angels)
Let His praises ring
Throughout the Heavens
La La La La La La
Da Da Dahhhh
Key oh co jay day may

They're dancing and singing
On streets of Gold
Singing of His Glory
Kay Jay nay Me Nay
Ta Ra Ra Boot te aye
Ta Ra Ra Boot te aye

Meet with Him
In the morning sunlight
La La La La La La Lahhhh   III I II
Ta Ra Ra Boom te aye   III I II
Ta Ra Ra Boom te aye   III I II

Da Da Dah Dah Dahh Dahhh

Ta Ra Ra Boot te aye
Ta Ra Ra Boot te aye

You are so good to me thank you for this song from Heaven and your Might and Power and Grace shed abroad to me every day. In Jesus Christ name, Amen.

WHEN HE SINGS TO ME APRIL 4, 2010

The Grace of God
Is Flowing
Down from Heaven
Two people are in love

Lift up thy voice and sing
Thank you oh Father

He is the Everlasting King
We bow down and worship
Upon the throne, The Lamb

All heaven and earth sings
Of His glory
His mighty arm outstretched
Over . . . .
All the earth . . . (slow progression)

In Purity and Majesty
His ways are known forever
Like the Mountains and the Sea
His hands outstretched forever
To give His joy and peace
To . . .   La
The ones . . .   La La
He loves   La Laaah . . . .

Thank you Father

THEY SING ALLELUIA TO THE FATHER MAY 12, 2010

All the angels in heaven sing alleluia

They love to cay around your banner Jehovah Nissi
They sing upon the wind
Alleluia
When the day is done they sing

Allelulia
When the morning comes
Alleluia
And now I say
That maybe someday
I'll be singing Alleluia before the throne
Mighty God you are worthy of praise
Thank you for today

You're welcome
get going

Kay da day boom
tinkle tinkle
Music in the city of God
going about the throne
in a high processional
of the angelic throng
Singing
Glory, glory to the Lamb
Praises to the adoring lamb
Sing hallelujah
mercy evident from the Lord Most high
Kay da day boom
tinkle tinkle

Got to go
Bye, bye
Oh Lord Just one more
Too late, Holy, Holy, Holy, is His name

Oh praise you Father, thank you for today
Oh worship you Mighty King
All glory to you today
Glorify your name Father.

Today
Bless them as they worship you
Singing a new song

Lord of glory
We love you-nothing
Answer to prayer is coming soon
You are most high
And have told the world
The way to worship
At the foot of your throne
You are the most holy God
There is none like thee
They sing in the heavens
They glorify thee

Glorify your name in all the earth—glorify your name
Glorify your name
Glorify your name in all the earth

Now Go!

<u>SOMETIMES WHEN I WORSHIP YOU GOD I WANT TO CRY MAY 16, 2010</u>

Worship your name Lord God
Worship your name
You are Lord upon the throne
The Most high and mighty God
Always there when I need you
Fairest Lord Jesus
Immanuel-God with us
Always there
When I call
Never leave nor forsake me
Morning light in my eyes
Miracles abound by your love

I love you Lord
Amen

HE IS HOLY 5/17/10

Bless the Lord
Bless the lord oh my soul
Bless His goodness throughout the day
Bless His holy name-loose
There is a name above all others
His name is Jesus
His name is holy

Hallelujah to His name

WHEN I THINK OF YOU OH LORD MY GOD, RIGHTEOUS ELOHIM IN HEAVEN MAY 24, 2010

Bless your name-loose
Bless your name in the highest
Bless those who praise you
Bless those who worship you
Bless those who come in your midst
And you give life to those who are hurting
I love you Lord
You are the strength of the nation
There is none like you
You are awesome
Alpha and omega
The mighty God
The morning star
There is none like you
The eagles' wings
The light on my face
My joy
The innocency in my soul
The fairness of every girl's hair
It all belongs to you
To be given glory to you
Worship, glory, honor power and praise to thee

Thou art allegation there is none like thee
None besides thee
You are Yahweh
YAHWEH

I AM THE LORD THY GOD WORSHIP ME

THE LORD JESUS CHRIST WAKES ME EVERY DAY MAY 28, 2010

The power of the Father is mighty
The power of the Father is mighty
He has everything in his arms
He's not like a man that he should lie
What He promises he will fulfill
His name is Holiness and Righteousness
His ways are truth and His mercies new every morning.
When I look to thee
You fulfill my needs
And allow me
To enter your courts with praise
In the morning light I will notice your name
And worship Thee
Saying thank you Father for another day
That I don't deserve
However His ways are Holy
And miraculous with great power
Holy One of Israel.
The Mighty EL
Anointed One, Prince of Peace

While you're watching me I am sleeping. Thank you Lord for another night. Allow me to see the light of day. Thank you for going ahead of me. When I see you I know that goodness and mercy shall sprinkle me with His grace.

Now go on . . . sleep! Rest! It is the time of day to work, be not weary in well-doing.

HOW I LONG TO WORSHIP THEE OH LORD MY GOD MAY 29, 2010

The atmosphere changes
When Jesus comes in the room
The blind man receives his sight as he calls on thee
And you listen to the man with the withered hand
And you touch these souls
Oh how I love you Lord
You cause the demons to flee
And the darkness to give flight
As you walk down the Galilee streets
Let me walk on the water with thee
Let me sing and worship thee
I call out your name when I needed a friend
I could not get over you've been there again and again.
When the shadows fall and the days get older
Then I will say "Lord take me."
You'll look at me then
When
I am ready
And lift my hand and say
Come away with me
Your home is ready
That you've wanted to see
All this time you've been patient to glimpse
What I've made for you after all your trials and tempt
I believe I've got someone waiting for you
She's wanted to see you, wanted you to know
How lovely the time you spent together
Bound together in love on His earth below.
She's waiting to see you
To welcome you in
Where you want have to give another sigh
As you rest before the throne of God

I wait for such a day
(You'll be there my lover)
I want it to be wonderful
(More than you know)

Take me Lord, I'm ready to go
When it's time . . . .
So ready . . .
I know, be watchful
Strengthen the things that remain.

God you are so good to me
I should not look at your robe
I whinny myself beneath your feet
Crying that you would hold me as before
As the way a man holds up his dear child
Happily like our Father in Heaven
Who loves us like the wind that praises
And mentions thee.

Now c'mon . . . .

Yes Father another day to worship thee

<u>WHEN THE VINE (JESUS) COMES TO ME 5/30/10</u>

If I stay in the Vine
I will be free
If I stay in the Vine
His life in me

If I stay in the Vine
Of the Lord my God
I'll have life and Joy
He gives without abandon
da da da ah dah ah da da da   dah dah da da

La la la la la la la la la   lala lala   la lah la

WHEN HE COMES TO ME IN THE NIGHT TIME (JESUS CHRIST) 5/31/10

They sing the song of the Lamb
Praise, sing to the Lord Most High
He is wondrously upon the throne
His praises sing forever more
Halleluyah to the name
Of the Lord Most High
La La Lah Lah   Lahhhhhh

Holy Holy is the Name   Fast Pace-La La La Lah Ah Dah, dah
Creatures bow before thee
Lord Most High   La La Lah Ahhh
Holy, Holy is the Name   La La La Lah   Ah Dah Ah
Creatures Bow before thee Lord
La La La la lah La Lah

As I worship you,
Ah Da Lah Ah Dahh

You are Wonderful
The King of the Universe
The One who sits upon
The Throne
To say, I love you

Praise you Lord, you're so good to me

I'M COMING SOON JUNE 3, 2010

La La La Laaaaa La La
La La La La
La La La La
La Lah Lah Laaaaah

I'm Coming Soon
I'm Coming Soon
I'm Coming Right Now . . . ow . . . ow

La La La La La Lah . . . .
La La La La
I'm Coming Soon
(Whistle-I'm Coming Soon)

Thank you Father
You're Welcome!

A CALL OF GOD JUNE 5, 2010 ORDINATION OF AN APOSTLE

Fire falls down from the sky
When window open
An anointing
A washing to cleansing
My spirit feels free
I cling to your open toed sandals
Walking on the road
When two were speaking
And you explained it all
As they headed back to the city
I listened
They said you were alive
Then you called out to me
I fall before thee
Peter do you love me
Feed my sheep
Do you love me Peter
Feed my sheep
Simon son of Jonah
Lovest thou me?
Feed my lambs.
Don't worry
I know the hour
When I will come before thee
To take you home
Believest me they will take you to a place you don't want to go.

Bare all things, believe
And I will take you further than any man.
Do you believe me?
Yes

Amen.

<u>BLESS YOUR NAME FATHER JUNE 6, 2010</u>

Holy Spirit in heaven opens a door
His glory is evident throughout all creation
When ministers began the flame of His Holy Spirit descends upon them
I feel the fire of God within me
I don't feel the same any more
His features in Heaven
Are beyond our understanding
His glory is throughout all Creation
Worship your name Father
O worship you Lord Jesus Christ
Father we fall down and bow down before thee
That you would listen to us once again
You are so Holy
We cannot look upon themselves
The Heavens rejoice at your laughter
No one sees where the hoar frost live
Or when the winds are called
To swirl before thee
When nothing exist without your presence
And we fall down before thee
Oh Ancient of Days
There is none like thee
Amen

Father God, a million may fall at your feet then may I join them
And tell you in your ear
I love you.

<u>May I find you ready to come unto me!</u>

Oh God I am weak you are everything
Greatly to be feared, I bow before thee,
Oh Great One, Have mercy on my soulllllllllllllllllllllllllllllll
Oh God of Glory

Now GO!

WHEN GOD COMES AGAIN JUNE 7, 2010

Columns of smoke rise in the sky
When the army of the Lord advances
They move
Armies are coming
What to do Lord?
WORSHIP ME!
TELL ME HOW GOOD I AM
MAKE ME KNOWN TO THE NATIONS
DON'T HIDE ME IN A JAR
MAKE ME KNOWN THROUGHOUT THE LAND
I AM THE ONE THAT CAN ANSWER ANY PRAYER
TIME IS NOTHING TO ME
BELIEVE . . . TRUST . . . GIVE ME A SACRIFICE OF PRAISE

WHEN CHRIST WAS BORN JUNE 7, 2010

Thumpity Thumpity
Something's coming
Her feet over the distant ground
As angels sing of Mary's grace
her hair flows in the wind
Her heart singing
Rejoicing
The Holy child of God is within her
She's smiling
Lifting up her basket
He's coming soon
I can feel Him inside me
Growing
Becoming the Savior of the World

His birth
Signifying
The Father's Anointed love
God so loved the world . . . .

There are no words to express what I want to say to thee, only . . . thank you Yahweh.

Praise Praise to thee	Lah Lah da de
Wonderful thee	Dah da Dah de
Thou art my all	La La La La
So wonderful to me	la la La lee

CHRIST, THE CROSS, MY SALVATION JUNE 7, 2010

I feel my foot slipping
There is a an outcropping of rock
Straining to be free,
Letting go
To hold on to thee
His cross was
Measured by Roman men
Angry about the day what they had to do
Unconcerned about who it was that wore the robe
Unkind punching and hitting, feeling no shame
As the Savior walked, took our blame
Down the road when I couldn't see
They laughed they jeered as he passed by
I believe he saw you as he passed up the street
Saying "This is the Father's will that I die to give
The gift you wanted so desperately but could not
Purchase on your own."

I AM THE WAY THE TRUTH AND THE LIFE NO ONE COMES TO THE FATHER ACCEPT THROUGH ME.

YOU ARE TO BE BLESSED OH LORD JUNE 7, 2010

Bless your name father
Bless your name father
Let all heaven and earth rejoice-
Glad at the sound of your glory
Let them rest where your glory resides
We're fulfilled in your grace
Measured out by your loving-kindness

Let all the angels worship you
Let all the angels worship you
Worshiping you with high praise
Where praise comes from and where it will reside
And nothing more stands in your way
Of receiving all the glory, you so richly deserve
We are weak
You are strong
You are the mighty Yahweh
The Holy One
Whose arm makes and breaks
And gives life
We are but dust before thee
Our petitions like leaves on a tree
That, float up to Heaven

Give me grace oh Lord
Look toward my face once again
See me
See any unrighteous way within me
Cleanse my heart
Make me more like thee

I SAW THE LORD SEATED HIGH ABOVE THE THRONE JUNE 8, 2010

He looked like sapphire
I couldn't imagine how
Beautiful he could be
Then I looked at His face
And wondered about my unclean state
Then He let me see His glory
He was magnificent
He showed where I could find relief
No one else knew how they could help me.
It was God's grace that found me just in the nick of time.
I couldn't have gone any further
Until He picked me up
You see that le . . . .

I AM THE RISEN LORD JUNE 8, 2010

Da   DaDaDa   DaDa

La   LaLaLa   LaLa
La   LaLaLa   LaLa

I AM the risen Lord
Lord Of Heaven & Earth
Lord Of Heaven & Earth

I AM your savior God
Lord of everything
Lord of everything

I AM the risen Lord
I AM the Holy God of Abraham
I AM the Holy God of Abraham

I bring joy and life and peace
To all who know my name
To all who know my name

TELLING DEATH TO GO AND FLEE IN CHRIST JESUS HOLY NAME JUNE 8, 2010

La La La La Laaa Laaa
La La La La Lu

Key et tay lah day dee
E tay ah day cah (Clap faster then faster)

Le may kay sha day
Key aye ma de du
To me key sha day
Le may key they do (clap, shout like tape recorder)

WHEN I WANT TO COME TO YOU EARLY IN THE MORNING GOD JUNE 9, 2010

Bless your name father through the blood of Jesus
Bless your name father
You are like refreshing water
That seals the distance thoughts
That, come against us
You are like the rush of the sea
That rushes over me
Overflowing me, taking me
Oh take me Lord
Never let me go
Continually wash over me

Bless you Father
You are like the fresh air and the breeze
Summoning me
Saying let's go outside
You've been cooped up inside
And I can give you new thoughts
As I was you clean in Christ Jesus Name.

Song-Nothing but the blood of Jesus,
    Oh precious is the flow
    That washes white as snow
    No other fount I know
    Nothing but the blood of Jesus

YOU LOOKED FOR ME WHEN YOUR HEART WAS HEAVY JUNE 11, 2010

Thank you God for this morning, Thank you God for life
And waking me up
You didn't have to, thank you kindly dear one
You are the mountains that I see
The joy of heaven I breathe
I can't go a day without you
Don't go away from me
Even when I am not what I am suppose to be
Have mercy on me
That you can receive all the glory
From the words and the worship of thee
Put not my foot on the dangerous path
But where I can walk next to thee
Let me see your love as it shines around me
When I'm looking at what I lost
To see the advantages of the gains you've given me
I'm not the same man
I need to draw close to thee
When times are difficult to see
Then by your raised arm
I will know your love for me

A Merry Christmas

LET ME WORSHIP YOU LORD JUNE 23, 2010

Your angels around the throne
Around the throne
Around the throne
Giving you glory

Worshiping as never before
To see your face
To see your glory
Like no other
You are powerful Jehovah Yahweh
Worship your name-loose hallelujah
You provide
How can I not praise you more and more.
Angels of mercy
Angels of grace
Lead me to the Holy place

HIS GLORY IS EVIDENT THROUGHOUT ALL CREATION JUNE 23, 2010

E shinay
The power of God is falling this morning—(He gives)
If you had seen the day began
You would have seen the angels making a way
For your blessing when you were thinking about the one
That you might have
You must listen to me
And stop the worship of the female form

Come on
Let's go

Thank you Father

A MILLION VOICES SING PRAISE TO JESUS CHRIST THE KING JUNE 24, 2010

A million voices sing
Praise to Jesus Christ The King
A million voices sing
Talk of the joy that he brings
A million voices sing
*add verses

La Lah Lah Lah
La Lah Lah Lah
La La La La Lah Lahhh

La Lah Lah Lah
La Lah Lah Lah
La La La La Lah Lahhh

Thank you Father for the song today

IF PRAISE WOULD RISE TO THEE JULY 15, 2010

I exalt thee
I exalt thee
I want to give my whole heart to thee
When I can't see you are in the midst of me
I exalt thee
I worship you another day
I must get in your presence
There is no other place to abide
Where Jesus Lives
Where God resides
His Spirit falls upon me
When I close the door
Only you around me
Lord I want more
Don't stop what you're doing
Let it continuously flow
Break down all my resistance
Until I'm wholly yours
Seeking to come before that place
Clean before you Holy one
By the blood of the Lamb
I take my place in Heaven
Before the glassy sea
In worship and adoration
As I bow unto thee

Thank you Father God

CONSIDERING THE CROSS IS THE WAY WE SHOULD GO JULY 15, 2010

America, America,
God shed His grace on thee
When His eyes look about may
He give His love to thee.
We need you Lord
We have gone astray
We can't find our way back
At the end of the day
We can't seem to come to the throne room
Like we use to do
Wholly in adoration before you
We lost the understanding of what
You called us to be
The darkness surrounds us
At the end of the day
And we need to understand
How to come home . . . to thee

It's your amazing grace dear Lord Jesus that I can see another day and I say thank you.

IN CHRIST JESUS YOU WILL FIND EVERYTHING YOU NEED JULY 15, 2010

I don't always say thank you like I should
I don't always tell you how wonderful you feel to me
But I want you to know that I can't do it without you
Move another step
I can't seem to lift myself
When I wake
Only you can do it
When you lift your hand
And tell me to
Rise up in the morning
And thank you
Thank you Lord

Thank you for another day
For waking me and giving me life
Listening to my prayers
Anointing me to write
To tell others of your holiness and goodness
And listen to their cares
Then telling them Jesus
Has a robe you should wear
Of righteousness
Believe me if you confess your sins to Him
He'll take away the sadness and leave behind the joy you seek

Thank you for another day and wanting to be more like you.

Worship the name of the Lord
You have more to do in this life
You can't give up that wish
That dream you brought to me
I want you to have it
So you can see my glory
And believe that
"I AM THE LORD THY GOD"
No one has seen the trouble
That you have been going throughout
They don't know the distance you walk
At night when your legs will not go another step
They can't hear you when you lie and wait for me
To heal your body
I know child I've been there
When you didn't know
Sometimes I have to give you a season
When times are dark
For you to see me in a more powerful way
You think you can't stand it
That I have forgotten you
However don't you know
That I'm making you to be
My answer to prayer for those around you
When you look in their eyes you see so much hurt and pain

When you call out and say "Jesus help them!"
Why shouldn't I use you?

I know it's hard
Wait a minute-It's almost over
I can't get you to stand
If you don't crawl first
There is a time coming
When this will be a light and momentary memory
You will wish to see
To tell others
What I made you to be

(Thank you Jesus)

Now you know why I put you through the paces
It hurts I know
When you wash and peer at your face
Wondering what is this accomplishing
For me
Don't be dismayed
It's all working toward my glory and an
Exceedingly great reward for thee

(Thank you Father)

I know what they say
When they pass by
I know about what you're thinking
When the joy leaves your eyes
Don't forget I've chosen you my child
To bare my name before all the Nations
And this is just part of the process
With consequential endeavors that this process
Will strengthen you for what is ahead
Trust in the Lord with all your heart, lean not to your own understanding
And in all your ways acknowledge him and he will direct your paths.

Thank you Father, thank you for showing me that. Hollowed be thy name.

ANTHEM FOR THE PARK THAT DAY

I know when I look to the clouds
The Lord will hear my voice
Then will I listen
And tell Him how I feel
And left the ministering Holy Spirit and angels
Fill my heart with His love

(FOR RESTORE THE NATIONS-PHILLIPIANS 2:6-16 FOR POLICE AND MILITARY)

I KNOW I NEED YOU LORD JULY 18, 2010

La La la lala
Lord takes care of me
La La la la la
La La La La La
I need you
lah La la
I know you and
Lah la la la
You died for me

WORSHIP HIM JULY 21, 2010

Angels abounding singing grace and glory to God
Father I hear the voices of mercy calls
To the room by the blood shed for us all
Glory, Glory to your holy name.
Bless, mercy infinite by the one whose always the same
Lord you are, you come to me
Lord the God of heaven I sing
Glory Glory
To the lamb
Amazing grace
To you I am
All God the while we sing to thee

Jesus my God
Holiness to Thee

l ll l
lll
l ll l
lll
l ll l
lll
l ll l
l   l   laaaah.

LIFE WITHOUT JESUS IS PRETTY BORING
JULY 22, 2010

I felt God tell me   La Lah Lah da Lahhhhhh
I felt the answer come   La Dah Da Da Da Dahhh
I knew when God told me
You are my Chosen One
To spread the Gospel   La La Lahhh La La
Throughout the Land   La La La La La La

And in my hour of sadness
When you come to me
Then I saw your hand
It set me free

And though I Am surrounded
By enemies on every hand
I know you with lift me
So that I can stand.

Only you Lord could know what I am going though and help me (In a present help). I need you Father, I can't do this by myself. Thank you. I appreciate all you do for me and who you are. I live for you an as answer to all I do in the future by Christ. Amen.

WHEN SHE COMES JULY 22, 2010

Calligraphy duties written on the wall
Inscribed forever by men with much usage
They are trying to say
She 'll come to you soon

Merry Christmas . . .

I'll see her and bless your holy Name Father

WHEN WE SEEK HIM WE WILL FIND HIM JULY 22, 2010

You are God and there is none other like thee dadada dada dada dah da dahhh ah-da
The Holy One who can see the inner part of me
Where can I hide?
Where can I hide?
Where . . . can . . . I . . . hide . . . . ?

You are righteous there is no other like thee
You are righteous there is no other like thee
Here He comes
Here He comes
The Holy One that we will see

His name is Jesus
The Alpha and omega
His name is Jesus (Higher registry)
The Alpha and Omega
Holy One of Israel you will see

I NEED YOU TO WATCH OVER ME LORD JULY 22, 2010

I am the way
I am the way
Of righteousness

I keep you safe
Whenever there
Is darkness

WHEN THE FIG BLOSSOMS THEN THE MASTER COMES JULY 22, 2010

The water is flowing over my soul
When August temperatures loom in the present
When features change and the Sun gives lessons
Then darkness abides and people seek
The knowledge of the God on high
When we seek Him.

Windshield washing
Late at night
I need to know you more
Will you let me in?
Even though there is pain and suffering
Oh both sides
His on the cross
Yours in different aspects of man
Social studies are what we need to know
To understand where we need to grow
To look out at the

WHEN A WOMAN PLEASES ME JULY 23, 2010

It was a cloudy day in spring when I saw
A love of my life
She was as comely and ruddy as a snowflake
Like a beanpole, marshaled with a transparency
That stuck to our minds, devoted to her every need
A woman that has lifted her skirt to her lover
A seed is planted and her garden grows into a vineyard of
Collected sighs
And she gives four other children, that listen to her voice,
Then you sing
A written song

That magistrates to all that go away and say
You are loved

Thank you Jesus, you are like a bridge over troubled water, I want to love you more and go deeper to see you as you are. How wonderful you are there is none like you.

YOU ARE HOLY JULY 30, 2010

You are Holyyyyy   la la lah ah lahhhhhhh
Almighty God   Da Da Dah
Everlasting Father   Da Da Da Da
Prince of Peace   Dah Dah da-ahhhh

You are Holyyyyyy
Soon Coming King
Wonderful One
Majesty On High

You are Holyyyyyyy
The Lord Jesus Christ
Upon the Throne
Seated with God

You are Holy, You are Righteousness, Justice and Peace. When I need you I sing and you come.

YOU ARE WONDERFUL GOD OF HEAVEN JULY 30, 2010

Merry Christmas.
I'm going into my blessings
Hallelujah
Worship the Lord

I hear His voice
Angels anoint me today
To teach His word
Through His word

Hallelujah
The Lord has come today
And set me free from the
Chains and strongholds
That had me bound

Set me free, You are so good to me
I don't know why you continue this way
But I thank you from
The bottom of my heart
Lord and savior.

Hmmmm, if I could only worship you for a thousand days and say how great you are. I still could not sing enough of you. You are awesome in this place oh God.

YOU ARE AN ANGEL WHEN YOU LOOK AT ME IN THE RIGHT WAY AUGUST 12, 2010

The grace of God
Like diamonds and jewels that came down from the cross (when he hung there)
let your grace come down from the cross
reign on us your blessings
From feet pierced for our sins
Hands that pour out love from being nail pierced
A crown filled with thorns as his head was wiped clean of blood
As riches came out of His side for us torn by a spear
They cascade down from the cross
The ankles turned bearing the balls inside like painted
Pearls that are at heaven's gates
We see His eyes crowned with tears of glass like transparent
Streets of gold in Heaven
No one else can tell what He heard as
His mouth tasted vinegar and His Ruby red tongue suffered
His body ripped like leaves of gold that purchased me
I didn't deserve it
He did it
Purchasing my pardon like a man purchasing a precious jewel

In settings of silver to present me as a gift purchased in the finest
Gold that I might have the greatest joy on the day I am presented to
His Father in Heaven
With a table adorned for our pleasure
Through the blood of His Son that flowed out like the finest wonder
We drink in goblets of life not the wrath reserved for those who are
unbelievers
In the Kingdom
Of God
Bring gifts to Him
Let Him drink of your love
Until He gets His fill and more
As we rejoice at His kindnesses
That are extended forevermore
Forevermore

La kay day me ah la nay key don ee la kah dah
Forever father we will be with you
you are awesome we want no more
It is life being with you

Thank you Father for the Son and for giving us this poem
For your glory
Through the Son
Amen.

WHEN I THINK ABOUT HIS GOODNESS, WHAT HE DID FOR ME? AUGUST 13, 2010

A mighty measurement was given
When Christ Jesus died for me
When all around Him were singing
The song of misery
Jesus Christ came out the grave
And gave them there the ones below
Freedom to be saved
I don't know why He did it-all for me.
Enduring kindness on the tree
When none believed in me

Just a thief that couldn't see
The wonders of His grace
Until He
Took my place
And hung there and died for me
Amen

Thank You Lord Jesus Christ for this poem and song for you

YOU MUST HURRY I HAVE A LOT FOR YOU TO DO TODAY AUGUST 14, 2010

Yahweh is doing something new and great in the Earth
And statue of judgment written over stone
A Kingly rule
A mighty man of God
Is doing the work of an evangelists
But the time is come
That he must began to teach them
The way of salvation
Many know why but they don't comprehend I need them to come in
So many are being lost
Destroyed because of a lack of knowledge
They can't see the harm that they
They don't listen anymore
Liken to a tree that moves
Then sheds it's leaves
Causing great harm
Doubtless to say they won't live again
Why did they leave the way of salvation
Tell them to return home soon . . . very soon
Be at peace
In Christ Jesus

Thank you Father I appreciate that
You're coming soon

"I Know."

I CAN'T BE ALONE WHEN I AM WITH YOU
AUGUST 14, 2010

Worship your name Lord
Thank you for so much for all you're doing
I can't even thank you enough
And say it
My heart is to afraid I'll become so emotional I can't stop
When I think of your grace
how good you are to me
I just can't imagine
Anyone better than thee
Thou art wonderful
Filled with wonderful kindness, grace and strengthen
Who can thunder or has an arm like you,
No one
You alone are yahweh
The Lord of Heaven and Earth
I am your servant
Amen.

Father thank you Lord for another day. I appreciate all you do. In Christ Jesus name.

IT TOOK ONE WHO REALLY LOVED ME
AUGUST 26, 2010

Worship the Lord
With your mouths open la La Lah lahhh
Give Him grace And the Honor he deserves
When you worship Him
Believe and you will receive
I saw you and I knew what you did
When they spoke out against you
they picked up stones to stone you
And I looked away and wrote on the sand
Unwilling to be tempted by mortal manifestations I called you aside and said
Where are thine accusers

"I don't know" you said
Then I said to you
"Go and sin no more!"
You looked at me twice
Then left that place
As I stood up
They looked at me
And told me
It can't be
I looked at them and said
I didn't come for those set free
but the ones who are bound
The ones . . . who need me

Amen. Thank you Father for your kindness in sending your son the greatest gift and then telling us about thee. Awesome God I worship thee. Amen, in Christ name.

Thank you lord worship your name.

Now go.

SEEING WHEN ANSWERS ARE COMING BY HIS WILL SEPTEMBER 16, 2010

Enter His Holiness
And hear of His goodness
the world is His
All belongs to Him
Now bow before the Lord
Worship His holy name
Enter His Presence with praise, singing and Thanksgiving
Marshal your thoughts towards Him and praise His holy name
Believe that I can do all things
And you shall see me differently
Stop wishing for man's change
I Am your Lord and Savior
There is no other besides me
"Now go!"

HIS NAME IS HOLY AND RIGHTEOUS AND WHEN WE SING ANGELS COME 9/19/2010

Bless your name above the nations
Let the Holiness of God flood to all cities in our midst
As did once the nations feel His Presence
And knew He was God
Yahweh the Lord of Heaven and Earth-your
He is kind to all who seek Him
Who want to know His name
He is gentle as a snow white dove
Listening and cooing-His grace to thee
The Lord
The Most High God is in this place
Holy, Holy, Holy
Lord God Almighty
You are Holy
And the reason for my life
My hope, my joy
To live a life worth living
To feel your grace
Immeasurably set upon a brow
Of the One who loved me the most
Thank you Jesus, Holy Lamb of God
Father of allegation
We kneel before you and thank you
And worship at your feet
Oh Most Holy God
Besides you there is no other

Give God the glory

Oh worship glorify your name now and forever more
Behold the Master Of Israel
Who is, Who was, Who will be
What He wills to be
I bow before thee righteous Father

Worship your Name Oh Lord, Hallowed Be Thy Name Forever and ever and ever. Amen.
Now go!

BLESSINGS, GRACE AND GLORY COME FROM THE LORD SEPTEMBER 28, 2010

Maker of heaven and earth
The skies bow down to you
The seas roar
And the mighty men fall
When they see your face
When they listen to your voice
And hear
The calming sound of the wind
I can feel your
They sing to you each day
Holy Father in the spirit
And His Word goes forth without being void
When the music sings in the spheres
Yahweh
They say again
Yahweh, The Lord of all
I listen, then sing to Him
They listen
And choirs move in sweet adoration of
Yahweh
Bless His Most Holy name.
Yahweh
He stood upon the mountains
Holder of the seas in His right hand
Maker of man
Hearer of their prayers
When they cannot see in the distance
When worries come
When we forget
He controls each of our steps
When we call to Him

Yahweh
Blessed to say His name
Worship the name
Hallowed be thy name
Sacred and Holy are you
My Father
Yahweh

Key shaelm may shhhhhhh
Holy is His name
Holy is He

Key . . . . (Angels are speaking) Holy
All you need to know
He is Holy, Holy, Holy

Bow down before Him
Halleluyah
Glory be to His name
Holy One of Israel
Bow down . . . . now
Amen

salad dressing ideas
Clover Leaf fields
Spinach dressing
Leaves of Gold salad dressing
Time to finish
They are waiting,

Tell about what you saw in heaven

A MORNING IN LOVE WITH GOD
OCTOBER 24, 2010

Angels dancing
People speaking of his grace
Angels speaking of his love for you
Free without cost

As they worship Him all the day
Myriads of the heavenly hosts
Walking down ladders
Bringing good news of His grace
That influences all creation
On this Sunday morning

Thank you Father God
For another wonderful day
Of praise

WISDOM, UNTERTANDING OF HIS WAYS
DECEMBER 3, 2010

Angels are missing
Thrown from above
Down on the Earth below
Where men dwell

To tell them
About their evil deeds
While listening to see
If man will fall into sin

However, God has put His Son on the earth
To take us up
Where Heaven be
That he came to set us free.

God is wonderful
They sing all the day
His name is wonderful
In a thousand ways.
Bridging the gap of
Internal woes

HOLDING GOD'S HAND DECEMBER 7, 2010

Poetry of a woman in love
Sometimes it's not for her
But for me
Touch
Instills hope
It's going to be okay
I need you
Summers coming again
I see you the manifestations believe me
He's going to take your pardon
Don't receive what they say
Believe in me
I've kept you this long-
I won't let you go
Trust and believe me (Angels are around you blessing you) (Thank you
Father God in Jesus' name
Amen).

I KNOW HOW YOU FEEL, MY LOVE
DECEMBER 8, 2010

Angels are around you
They know how you feel
When you look in the glass
And read
Yet you don't see Anything changing
It was the same way for me
I saw it
The other day
You came home wondering
Will I ever be
The man I want to be
To feel your hand in mine
Knowing it's okay careful for the tears
You try to make stay away
I feel you my child
I just need you to breathe

I know how you feel
I haven't gone anywhere
When you hear the wind
Angels are singing to thee
I'm here
I haven't gone anywhere
It's different you know
Sometimes you have to look closer
To see
What I'm making you to be
You are mine child
I didn't leave your presence
You asked me
You said I want to get nearer
And I heard you
Don't be afraid
I'm almost done
You were about
To believe his lie

Don't fail to come near me Lord Jesus
Your promises are true
I know who I am
I know I'm in need of you

Thank you Lord Jesus Christ
Thank you Holy Father
Immaculate Holy One,
Anointed King
My everything, My all,
The King of Kings
And Bright and Morning Star
Who knows me so well.
I believe

THIS MORNING I WANT TO GIVE YOU A NOTE OF PROMISE, THAT IF YOU TAKE THESE WORDS TO THE PEOPLE AND SAY THEY WILL BE BLESSED IF THEY LISTEN THEN I WILL GIVE YOU THE ANSWERS YOU SEEK. BELIEVE THE PROMISES OF GOD. HIS BLESSINGS ON YOUR NATION, AMEN.

WHEN MY KNEES BOW TO THEE

Jesus and America
Run to thee naked
Tare off all we wear idols etc

When Jesus saw America, she was a child not yet grown
Small and tender with no one to care for it
Then He took it in His arms and loved the one no one wanted
Shadows increased and years pass by then we turned away from thee
And saw others who gave us lies and we no more wanted thee
They made us feel that you were of cruelty
But in our sin and ungodliness we didn't listen to thee . . . and suffered

Jesus, we America have sinned,
Let us run to thee naked
Tare off all the idols we wear
Help us so we desire thee again,
To look into your face,
Let angels minister to us,
Draw us back
Tug on our heart strings
The iniquity in our souls, purge us,
Free us from thoughts of destruction and inadequacy
Bring us back to the floor in a place of meeting
We need you
Open our understanding
Make us your bride
Traverse the way according to your lovingkindness
Mend our hearts
Align us back with your heart beat help us to hear
Forgive
Flood in the lostness of our ways
Teach us to lean on you
Supply depending, drinking from your breast
We need you oh Lord
We still can't do it by ourselves
we need you
Don't turn away like a mother that leaves her child, and turns away
Look on us we had sinned and done unrighteousness

But hear us, listen to our cry, like the daughter virgin of Jerusalem help us
We are ashamed of our ways, we need you to take us back,
Hold me once again that I will forget my backslidings
Let your love be shown in such a great way we will fall on our knees and worship and praise you.
Flood our hearts
Keep us from guile
Cleanse us
My people do shame and evil
Their ways are known to you but if we, (I) go out to them and tell them of the multitude of your kindnesses,
Then they will hear, consider and seek your face
Let your words teach and instruct the hearts of the wicked
Until the mighty worship thee
Tell us your ways so we can see your majesty
Then fall and kneel before thee oh soon coming King
Have mercy
And father those who deceive and cause others to fall in this nation
Show them your Light that burns through the darkness of their minds
Let them not seek your face, lead them where they need to be in causing others to stumble
Lead them back to the light
Father they cause us to fall, injurious ways.
Know our hearts, they seek evil-all the day they plot evil and the demise of the promises you gave to this nation.
Remember your joy at besetting us with your crown jewels
Bring us to our knees in humble contrition
We are not like the other nations, they know you in ways of knowledge but we are your children, we see your face
Don't give us the filth that clings to us
Wash us new
Take away the Princes, prophets, shepherds that take away our focus away from thee and restore the sight that we may see
Our media worships at the altars of decaying idols, we wickedly consider the ideas we see on screen with the idolatry in Los Angeles, take away our sin, show us the righteous considerations of truthfulness and going to the poor and destitute.
We have become fat, prideful, and need you to take away the senseless arguments of human logic that lessens what you consider Holiness.

Be kind listen to the voice and cries on the altars of women crying but to thee and children saying prayers,
Hear their hearts let us not turn from thee.
Listen to our heart beat . . . Jesus, Jesus, Jesus,

Give us contrition to go throughout the nations of the world to tell them your laws and statues and the judgment to come.
Hear our prayer oh Lord, deliver us not into the hand of our enemies because they are many
Have mercy and deign us to call all nations to become more like you and worship your name
Let Israel praise you when we sing to you and join them like a sister holding her little brother that you have given us. Our little brother needs you Yahweh Father, through the blood of the Messiah Yahshua,
help us to keep faith and touch his hand when he is bleeding and always protect the glory you've given him. Let us never shy away from our duty and to be a good sister that hears when he cries and makes sure he is well. Forgive us
We are but sheep without a shepherd, Holy Ghost come into our nation, with contrition let us call out to thee, set us aflame to seek you out-Holiness.
The cankerworm and filtiness of our fornications have harmed and taken away the beauty you gave us,
Help us to look to you and rise up to say, "Jesus." I know you love me, I need your help as the nation of America, help us oh God,

We love you Father
Our hearts give you honor and glory
Your name is holy
And we lend our lips in praise to thee
Let America sing halleluyah
Open our voices to sing
Of your grace

Magnify your name oh Lord
When we seek thy Holy face
Our divisions are many
We let go of opportunities
When you have told us what to do Light a fire beneath us

THE THANK YOU SONG (JOLLY TUNE TO DANCE TO) 1/7/2011

Thank you
Lord my God
Thank you
Lord my King
Thank you
Holy One
You are Lord of everything

da da
da da da
da da
da da da

daaaa da
da da da

da da da dah dah dah dah

You are
My Father God
I worship
I praise you
Thank you
For keeping me
My Lord My God My everything

It Has Been
A lovely day
He has given me
Words to say
I thank you for
Using me
To touch lives in worshiping

Merry
Am I inside
A life giving
Wall of faith
To build a way
To see me
When you stand in eternity

La La
La La La
La La
La La La

Laaaa La
La La La

La La La Lah   Lah Lah Lah

Holy is
The Lord our God
In majesty
He reigns on High
You are
The Holy God
Awesome in praise and wonderment

Awesome in praise . . . . and . . . . wonderment (Slowly, phrase each word,)
Da, da Da   Da   Dah da dah

After song.(praise Him)

You are Holy
Magnificent are you
We worship you in this place
We adore and worshiping
We call on your name to
Bring us closer to the
Executive Suite in Heaven

MY WIFE'S SONG FAITH TO BELIEVE
JANUARY 5, 2011

By faith all things are possible   dada da da dadadada
All things are possible   lala la lalalah
If you have faith to believe   lalala lah lahlah
All things are for you   dah dah dahhh dahhhhh

All things are possible   lll l ll
All things are possible   lll l ll
It's just a matter of time   lll l ll
Until you will see   lala la lala
The evidence of His grace   dah dah dah
To all who believe   la la . . . la . . . . la . . . lahhhhh

By faith all things are possible   dada da da dadadada
All things are possible   lala la lalalah
If you have faith to believe   lalala lah lahlah
All things are for you   dah dah dahhh dahhhhh

HIS KINDNESS EXTENDS THROUGHOUT THE
UNIVERSE (PSALM 19) 1/25/11

The angels sing hallelujah
Another day has come
The Master's grace
Has touched again
Saying Hallelujah
It's morning
It's morning
La LaLa   La La La La
La LaLa   La La La

La LaLa   La La La La
La LaLa   La La La

Boom Tah Boom Doom Doom Doom
Boom Tah Boom Tah Doom Doom

La La La La   La La
La La La La La

Music strings from Heaven
As the Angels sing
Hallelujah Master

Awakening everything
We don't see it as kindness
When we are awoke
We worry to much about the day
And say I must get up and go

Oh Hallelujah
If we worshiped Him
Then joy would be evident
In the things we say

LaLa LaLa   LaLaLaLaLaLa
LaLa LaLa   LaLaLaLa

Quiet morning
Hear His Breath began
Awake oh Daniel
Live another day

Messenger texting In My Soul
Something I have to do
Marriage is sweetness
I hope I'm there with you

IT'S WONDERFUL TO BE NEAR YOU AGAIN, JESUS 2/16/11 GOD, THANK YOU FOR WAKING ME TODAY

Thank you for the morning lightnings
Thank you for your love
Early in the morning do I seek thee
You awaken me to the dawn
And I live and breathe again

Like a man on a ship
Waiting for the wind
Thank you for giving me life again
And allowing me to breathe
I have to have you in my life
This morning light flows into my brain
I just praise you for another day

My soul and my heartbeat are yours
Another day, another hour to seek your face
Thank you for your glory that shines all around me
The spiritual nature within me reaching out to you again
It's wonderful to be near you again, Jesus.

I AM HOLY 3/31/2011

Thou art Holy Oh Lord
You are Holy   Da Da Da Dah

You are the Righteous One   Da da Dahh da dada dah
Lord upon the throne
You are Holy

Holy
To the Master of Creation we sing
You . . . are . . . Holy . . . .   La . . . . ah . . . . Lah ah La . . . .

Thank you Father, You are Holy

OH JESUS YOU ARE MY KNIGHT IN SHINING ARMOUR APRIL 2, 2011

Glory honor, power to your name	La La La La La La Ta Da
Lord we worship thee	Dah De Da dee Deeeee
Glory honor and power to your name	La La La La La La Ta Da
Lord we worship thee	Dah De Da dee Deeeee
You are the Father Of Lights	Doo ah da da da da

We sing

We bow

Lord of Lord and King of Kings

To thee we . . . . sing

da dah

da dah

Dah ahhh Dah e Dee de dee

Dah ahhhhhh La Dahhh

Hallelujah in the Heavens

Praise and Glory be

To the Author and Finisher of our faith

There is none like thee

There is . . . . none . . . . like thee . . . .

WHEN I LISTEN IN THE MORNING I HEAR THE ANGELS SINGING 4/4/11

Almighty God, the Everlasting Father,   La . . . La Lah . . . . La Lah Lah

Alpha and Omega, The Prince of Peace,

Glory to The Lord On High   La La LaLa La LaLaLa

He is Holy

There is no one like you   La La LaLa . . . . Lah Lahhh . . . .

Oh praise you Father,

Let all praise come to you

Worship Him above the nations

Thank you Father, thank you for the angelic hosts

(A crowd in white and yellow, singing, wings up in the end, then they went back)

I WORSHIP THEE 4/24/11 RESURRECTION DAY

Before your presence I worship thee

WHEN I CALL OUT TO YOU APRIL 30, 2011

Dear Christine I love Jesus so much,

Sometimes I can't tell Him how much.

It's like jewels and diamonds fall on me

And I don't know how to catch them all at one time.

His Glory is amazing,
Anchors fall and my soul is redeemed, where I need to be.
Oh Thank you Lord, heal me, I am free.

SOMETIMES I THINK ABOUT THE LORD SO MUCH
APRIL 30, 2011

It's amazing
When I look into your eyes Lord And I see the beginning of the day
Not worried about Knowing, you have already fixed my way
Through doubts and storm that lay beneath me,
You have brought me out when I needed to see you
A crescendo arises in my heart
Love overflows when I need to start
To tell you
How much I care about you

You need none to tell you
And yet I try to say
How beautiful you are
And your love abounds
Despite all my heart's uncleanliness

Oh I want you so bad
I need to get down on my knees
My face to the ground
In humble adoration
When I seek your face

Your blood runs down from the cross
Arms yielded wide
As people take a stance
Standing in judgment
Of what they see
Not knowing this was the way
The father meant it to be
That Jesus might hang there for me
While taking my place
Where I should be

Caught in Satan's grasp
Listening to lies in my sleep
Unable to turn back when I felt His love
Steeped deep in sin
Unable to move
Calling out to you
JESUS save me
Please oh God, "SAVE ME!"
Give me life again
Take away my shame
Confessing my sin
In a moment to began . . . the transition
To You

CLOSE THE DOOR AND TALK TO ME

I don't know where I have been this morning
I don't know where I have been today
You called to me
When I was asleep
And I couldn't move
Wrapped in self-blaming
Thinking about myself
When all around me
I see where I failed
I didn't consider that
I might be in His plan
Thank you Father
In consequences to dark
You show me the way home

**This is why I talk to you so much Daniel
I love you.**

Oh Father worship your name, you are so holy and kind, remembering me
all my days

THIS IS MY GIFT TO YOU

Don't tell people I don't know you
When you look and their faces look at you in agony
Watching your eyes
They see a monolith but don't know how to access the God
You serve
They want you to be strong
Tell them the truth,
Give them life

I Listen to you
What you say
Telling them about you
What about me?
They need . . .
The One who can save them when they are crying
No one needs to know what you think
So butt out!
Let me talk
I Am, the Key
You get on your knees
And worship me now

My heart is hurting, angels be around me
Hold me in the Father's hand
I've done evil God

Now see my Face!
Judgment is coming
They need to know
Worse conditions are coming
I will see to it
That you are well taken care of
But when I call your name
There should be no hesitation
To do my will
Now get going!

Thank you Father, I needed this upbraiding. I didn't do your will wholly so I need to ship up and become the man you created me to be. Forgive me Father, Lord God of All. In Jesus Christ name, Amen.

WHEN THE MORNING SONG COMES APRIL 30, 2011

Stepping on stones of grace
Renewing each step I take
Moving out to where I want to be
There is an answer coming in the wind
Letting go of who I want to be
And listening
To you
As you tell me
To listen to you
Let go of distractions
And be
Who you created me to be
As I bow before thee

Bow before thee Father

WHILE I WAS IN A DREAM I HEARD YOUR VOICE CALL TO ME 4/30/11

Awaken from a dream
Internal images
He sees me
And wakes me
Another day
For His Glory
To shed abroad His kindnesses
And encourage others to see
Why I love Him so

Thank you Father God for another day

SONG FOR MARCHING BAND PRAISING GOD APRIL 12, 2011

Da Da Dump
Worship Of The Lord Almighty
Da Da Dah Dah
Da Da Dah
Dumpity
Dump Dump Dummmm

THE MAKER OF THE HEAVENS SONG APRIL 12, 2011

Eeeeh-Like mosquito Quick notes

WHEN I LOOK TO THE SKIES I SEE JESUS APRIL 12, 2011

La La La Dum

WHEN I LOOK I SEE JESUS JUNE 8, 2011

If we open the door,
To Christ The King
If we open to Him
We sing
If we open up the door
To Christ the King
Then we'll receive life
And the joy He brings.

La La LaLa Da Da Dahh
Da Daht Da Da
Da Da DahDah da da
Da Dah Da
Dah da DahtDaht da da Dah
La dah dant daaa-
Din din nada da
Da Da Do Ding Ding

Ii ii I II ii I I I
ii I I I I I iii
I ii I II ii I I I
ii I I I I I iii

Thank you Father for the song.

WHEN I REMEMBER HIS LOVE FOR ME
JUNE 14, 2011

I know the dance of the soul
While I was asleep it came to me
I was asleep and saw
An angel telling me to rise and dance
So I began to seek Him out
And listen to His voice
As He told me intuitively
To love Him with all my heart
And began to lift my feet
Then I would hear His voice
And dance with the King of All.

Thank you Jesus, when I remember your love for me, I fall down and cry.
Halleluyah thine be the Glory, Halleluyah.

THERE IS AN ANSWER WHEN YOU CALL
JUNE 14, 2011

I can't hold on
Is what you said
When you thought
I loved you no more
My Child
Don't you understand
I don't care about
All the column praises
How you want to be
Next to me in everything
I want you to seek me
And draw near
Then we can talk, commune and fellowship together.
But as soon as you leave
I'll be bridging the gap with my love
To bring you back to me

Thank you Jesus, thank you Father, you love me so much.

JESUS KNOWS HOW I FEEL JUNE 15, 2011

La LaLa   La La La La   La La La (Fast paced)
La LaLaLa   La La LaLa   La La La

Whenever you call on my name I will hear.
They are doing it now in Heaven
They are worshiping my name
Above all the heavens
Giving Him the honor
That's due His name.
Worship of His Lamb
The sweet refrain

Above the noise of the earth
You deceived me (The Enemy)
Offering a change
I listened and thought
The deception is true
Hears me call out
Telling about a substitute

Thank you Father for the words to this song.

LISTENING TO PETER'S CRY JUNE 18, 2011

I saw your face in the window sill
Sorrow was upon your brow
It didn't matter anymore

I saw your face
watching
As I passed by
Listening to the crowds

Then you stuck out your hand
Bring me vinegar water they asked
And put a crown of thorns on my head
It hurt.

But you didn't say anything
You put dice on a robe
And took what I was wearing-your win

I sat down among by the fiery place
Then the cock crowed

Where were you on that fateful day?
I wish I had seen you
You say I will never leave you nor forsake you
But you went away when they whipped me with mangled iron in strips of
leather

No one came to my destiny
They all left
Then there was you
Sorrowful
Looking at the cross from a mangled tree
While you swung in the air

Father you were with me
As I looked up from the tree
Bridging the gap for them
To come to thee

Like a row of wheat in the summer
I was cut down
And yielded up the ghost

Why are you laughing now
The air is thick with darkness
But you deign to tell one next to you on the cross
He is set free from his sin

I believe
You are the Christ
You once said
The Son of the Living God
Now I see you afraid before men

Bowing unto their desires
Worried about what you are saying
What man can do to you
Only I can take away your soul,
Peter.

Will you get into the boat?
Will you walk on water with me?
Peter
Will you let me show you what can happen
When you give me your hand?
Worship me
That's all I ask
Tell them that "I love them."
I want them to know me
Teach them the way to become whole
Give them instruction to lead them to
Seeking me with all their hearts.
Then I will give you more to do.

Thus sayeth the Lord. Amen.
Thank you Father for your grace in showing me all that you would have
me to do.

WHY ARE YOU SO KIND TO ME JESUS?
JUNE 18, 2011

Why are you laughing now
The air is thick with darkness
But you deign to tell one next to you on the cross
He is set free from his sin

I believe
You are the Christ
You once said
The Son of the Living God
Now I see you afraid before men
Bowing unto their desires

Worried about what you are saying
What man can do to you
Only I can take away your soul,
Peter.

Will you get into the boat?
Will you walk on water with me?
Peter
Will you let me show you what can happen
When you give me your hand?
Worship me
That's all I ask
Tell them that "I love them."
I want them to know me
Teach them the way to become whole
Give them instruction to lead them to
Seeking me with all their hearts.
Then I will give you more to do.

Thus sayeth the Lord. Amen.
Thank you Father for your grace in showing me all that you would have
me to do.

<u>WHY ARE YOU SO KIND TO ME JESUS?</u>
<u>JUNE 18, 2011</u>

Watching you laugh
when the tomb was empty
seeing you smile
When I appeared to you
Watching your face in amazement
When I took the honeycomb and ate
When you saw me
When they said "He is risen."
You didn't want to believe
Oh doubting Thomas what must I do
To help you see
Touch me in the place where the nails went through

See where they put the spear in my side
Don't be faithless but believing
For blessed are those who have not seen and yet believe
Are you faithless?
Do I need to show up every time?
With every need?
Why don't you show me what you can do with the faith you have received.
Speak to the storm don't wait for me to tell you
Listen to them dribble
I know what they have need of before they ask
Where were you oh Thomas when I first appeared?
What happened?
Didn't you know I would be with you?
I'll never leave you nor forsake you
That's a promise.

When you told me you loved me, "I LISTENED"
I'll never forget what you said to me that day when your thoughts of darkness crashed about you
You were confused, staggering, struggling under the weight of your sins,
Burdened by thoughts
With no relief.
Then I came to you and saw you struggling bound by chords of dismal darkness
And I opened the door and you where free.
But have you forgotten the cost. What I paid for you?
A ransom that required my blood to be shed
Not a recording on a tape
But everything you owe me
So don't say you can't give me more than I ask
When I speak to you to finish the work each day
I'm a living example of how you can accomplish more than you ask or think with God's help.

Thank you Father for taking an example and teaching me never to give up.
Mercy and grace are in your hands.

ANOINTING TOUCH MY HEART JUNE 19, 2011

Song to be sung by Kari Jobe when she ask me

The darkness in my heart has gone away
The emptiness inside I can't feel anymore
I needed to get free but didn't know how
Until you came inside and changed me

It wasn't a day that I could hold in my hand
You listened to a woman a frighted by life she lived
That couldn't get up from the well
Until you passed by

The word came from your lips
And I was set free
The burden taken off from your release
When I looked into your eyes

There was love there
Not condemnation
As you reached for me
I needed you then

When I called my friends
I left you then
And walked a path along a stony road
That they might see
What the Messiah meant to me

I'm desperately in love with you
Making my way anew
Getting out of myself
That you might live in me

I know you want more of me
I'll open the door
Let me kneel beside you

Grant me the grace
A Holy anointing when I call on you

Thank you God for your presence and hearing my voice

WHEN YOU LOVE ME JULY 11, 2011

When I fall beneath your feet
I learn to breathe again
in the morning

When I see the look in your eyes
I to do the things that are righteousness
As the day goes by

You saw me in my need
And heard my morning cry
And you spoke to my heart-I love you

You're so good to me Father

THANK YOU FATHER JULY 12, 2011

Dear Father your angels where with me as I slept last night
they sung a song to me
In the peacefulness of your holiness
And I worship and thank you
It was like the joy of heaven came down
Thank you so much
I would be remiss not to glorify your name
And glorify your name even more
Thank you Father
Oh God you bring your heart to me
You are so good
Worship your name
Praise your name
Thank you for another day

You fill up my heart with love for people today
You love me
You care for me
I love you God
You are so good to me
(Angels hear and understand)

Thank you Father
Yahweh bless your holy name
Bless you Lord
With all that cries within me
Bless you Lord

In Christ Jesus name, Amen.

WHEN EVERYTHING SEEMS TO FALL DOWN JULY 13, 2011

They are working hard to find answers for you
While you worship me
Steady hands working behind the scenes
Teaching you

Thank you Father, in my life, your will be done

YOU ARE THE MIGHTY GOD JULY 18, 2011

Lord
I love you that's all I have to say
I feel within me a thousand songs to sing to you
A glance at your face to know you
On a desperate day in a desperate hour

Sometimes
The appearance of your grace
Can fill my heart again
When the rains have gone
And the storms subside
Left beneath
Your pierced blood side

From agony and pain
To the sublime love of your grace
Patiently waiting for me
Helping me
Watching me
Understanding me
Knowing me
Oh Father, what can I say but I love you

LET ME SING TO YOU JULY 18, 2011

Your angels bow
As I come into your presence
As they worship and say
Holy, He is Holy
And I look upon your face
Doors open before my eyes
I see you

Out of the depths of
The mountains, rivers and valleys
Of my soul
Let a song be sung to you today
As my heart beats
Let angels come out from that Holy place
And worship adore flood like a gushing river
From the valley of my eternal being
Never ceasing, ever preceding knowing
Of thee
Oh, Heavenly Father, I worship you

SHE WANTS TO HEAR YOUR VOICE LORD JULY 18, 2011

Come here child
Come here daughter
I'll take care of you
I hear your voice
I hear your cry

I'll shush your tears
Make your heart cry
In love to me again
Speak my darling
Tell me what you need

"Daddy"

I hear you daughter
I'm here
Speak to me
Tell me what you need
Where you're at?
Where you want to be?
I'll know
Just tell me what's on your heart
What can I do for you?
You are wonderful God

I NEED TO BE NEAR YOUR THRONE ROOM
JULY 19, 2011

I needed you that day Jesus
More than I need you now
When it all fell apart
My world imploded
And you saw me crying
It felt like a thousand mirrors
All laughing at me

The house caved in
Then you saw me there
And you said
Come here my child

Rivulets of your love flowed to me
When I couldn't drink of your deep cistern
You prepared the way
For my soul to rise

When there was nothing left within me
Backed against a wall
That made me see
Your love

You looked into my eyes
And saw inside my heart
And made me feel good again
I could drink and feel free
Pleasant thoughts surfaced in my heart
As I neared your throne room
Saying Jesus
Anoint me to do your will
Father, Father God I love you

Angels began singing Hallelujah

RESURRECTION SUNDAY JULY 19, 2011

You gave me something I didn't desire
Laying upon a stone
When they put you in the ground
When the rains fell
And the darkness cried to thee
You lifted me out of the tomb place
When you called my name
And said child arise

I laid there for a moment then began to breathe
To began again to listen
Becoming aware of your kindnesses
As my body began to move
My arms stretched out
To receive your love
And I listened
You wanted to know me
And I called your name
"Father"

Thank you Father for resurrecting my life

JESUS YOU ARE THE WAY JULY 20, 2011

Answered prayer
The hem of His robe
Pulling, tugging
Waiting for Him through the crowd
Dusty and dirty
Watching for a clearing in the crowd
To get to His feet
Remembering He held me once

When the song in my heart comes alive
Especially on the day
When He touched me
Daughter, thy faith have made thee whole
I'm clean
Well inside
No more pain and suffering

Miracles abound in the presence of your hands
Anointing of God filling the land
Hair tossed blowing perfect strand
Beneath His feet the immortal man
He hears my heart
When my thoughts aren't clear
He reaches out to me
So I can stand
Child your sins are forgiven, it was in my plan

When it really matters, God you are there

THE FIREPLACE JULY 20, 2011

Something has gone wrong inside me
I'm not the same man
That once worshiped you with all his heart
The one who would get up in the morning
I couldn't wait for the day to start
I looked out the window

At what you wanted me to be
And I fell in step
just to see your miracles

I loved you with all my heart then
I couldn't get enough of you
Wanting more and more
Until evidently you saw I wasn't backing off
And you propelled me
With the wonders of your grace

The lamp is now lit
But now the embers grow cold
Day is dying
Night is old
Circumstances surround me
A literal end
Prostrating before you again and again
Seeking solace
On a knee bend
Worshiping
Uncovering the old me
The one you want to know
Listening for the birds to sing a melody
Rhyme and reason to return to me
While I sing to you

Don't go away I still need you

CRYING OUT TO YOU JULY 21, 2011

My heart is wrapped up in you
Your blood was shed for me
The depths of your love increasing within me
The solace of anonymity no more
My heart beating
Endanger of bursting by your love and grace

Foundation Stones of my life
Which upon no other can build
Trophy in a case
Is my love for thee
Father of Lights
God who knows my weaknesses

Shower me with your love
Teach me your ways
Allow me to see you in a different way
Let me cry until
My heart is real to thee
And I know the price you paid

I need to be beside you

WHILE I SIT THERE WAITING JULY 22, 2011

A minute man
Morning sun running
Eagles flying in the distance
Causing me to turn and look around me
Understanding
The climatic changes and shifts in my heart

Going into places I've never been
Seeking you
I went inside your heart
At the deep recesses
And I looked around
Your rooms were empty
No quiet places
Just to walk outside and feel your grace
Is all that I needed

Listening to distinguished gentlemen
Fabricate a tale

Listening to the government saying all is well
Tender mercies that come down to me
Open the door flood the seas within me

Jesus you took my life apart
Sensed all my needs
Knew where to start
To repair my heart

Hollowed places inside
My reserved walls
You've pulled down
To cause me to look up to you
As I stand there alone and naked
Vulnerable
Emptying my last spool of thread
Near your door

Jesus help me

Thank you Father

WHEN SHE'S HOLY AND WORSHIPPING THEE
JULY 22, 2011

There is a woman that makes me feel different in life
She listens to the Lord
Becomes who God wants her to be
A rarefied treasure a jewel of love
Beseech-ed by His pardoned consumed by His love
Anemone soft sponge
That floats on the sea
Created in His glory
In untold passages of time
Formulated in His thinking long ago
To be his daughter
As we tried all things
And finally were restored to Him
The mighty God that

Awakens in the day
Walks through the seas
Were we long to be
Continually waiting
While the rivers part
Rifts in the valley
That call out to me
Distant courses of
Graduate degrees
Earnest intentions
We don't need
Just His love

You're wonderful to me
Father

MAY GOD'S HAND REST ON YOU JULY 28, 2011

Softly and tenderly Jesus is calling is a song I was singing the other day.
Just worshiping God, listening to His voice,
Learning where I'm suppose to be.
Systems of reason simply don't seem to be.
Occasional glances, curtains rise.
In the center of my hurricane,
Opening the mail.
Whispering Jesus be near.
When He answers I look beyond the rise.
I listen and the darkness that covers me recedes.
Formation of thoughts remain . . .
Of you.

When I call to thee, the angels consider me

WHEN SHE CALLS MY NAME JULY 29, 2011

Come with me child
I'm scared, I'm afraid
I know
Take my hand

Please don't let me go
I'm here
Please God show me where to go
It's not to far is it?
No, my child
Will we get there soon?
Almost
Thank you Lord
You're welcome

When you listen to my voice I am astounded

I HAVEN'T LEFT YOU ALONE CHILD JULY 29, 2011

Healing and wholeness
An open door to her heart
A cumulative romance
With the Creator of her heart
She listens to my voice
When I call her from sleep
She listens in the night
At the sounds of my waking song
She listens with her ears fully
Breathing
Lord I need you
When her mouth opens
Then I can feel her heartbeat
As she sweetly sings
I can't stand being without you God
The muscles in her neck ache
As she plays the flute
Her mouth stirs the notes
And she hears my voice
Play child, play on
Listen to those around you
And sing on the flute
Your heartbeat wrestles with the refrain
You wait

Listening for my directions
And the notes come to you
When you are finished
I clap my hands
Well done

You knew us when we were children to young to say so, we love you.

YOU ARE SO WONDERFUL TO ME JULY 29, 2011

Muscles straining
Your fingers on the chords
Hearts rending
Associated stanzas
On a sheet of music
You memorize
As they play
In time
While you sing
In your heart
The joy of God
Shown in the delight
On your face
I was made for thee

You heal all the secret parts of me

JESUS YOU SAW MY HURT AND YOU MADE A CHANGE AUGUST 4, 2011

You saw my hurt and pain
When I looked at her
And felt her sorrow
You heard my voice
When others looked away
Her sadness made my heart melt
Oh God I desire you more

You listen to her voice and saw her cry
I heard every tear in your eye
When you were surrounded with no one to help
I came when you needed help to get the box off the shelf

You look at her steady and wonder what she'll be
I see a man in an arena be
My song to the natives in foreign lands
Telling them how Jesus can . . . save them

I haven't forgotten you
I made your bed
While you were thinking looking around
Trying to figure out the beginning of the day
A need to be with me
Surfaced in your heart
And I listened to you
Read my word and you'll understanding
How to go about this day mere mortal man

Thank you God when you hear my voice.

I KNOW HIS NAME AUGUST 7, 2011

You are like a river inside my heart
That runs slow ebbing over my terraces
Flowing down into the deep inner cases
Toward my joy
When I hear your name called
If they could see me then
They would run to you
Heedlessly . . .
Desiring their souls also to be filled
To find the grace of life
In the darkest night
When nothing seems to be

When His Morning Light comes
Your face light with the dawn
Then I'll say "you're beautiful"
Then I'll know-His word has founded your frame
And you'll never be the same

His love is wonderful

ANGELS CALLING TO GOD WHILE YOU'RE SLEEPING AUGUST 3, 2011

Su Ba Yay Kee
Tay Nay Do
Keep me close to
Your heart
Oh Lord

Do dah dee dee
Tee Nah Dee

Oh Can (long a-Ca) Nee Kee
Can Nay Do Ta Do
Will you stay beside me

Lu May Te Day Nee
Cay an Nay do
Do you wish me to be

Jah nee Myyyy
Kee Nay At Tow
Lay dah
While I sleep you watch over me Lord Amen.

Praise and thank you Father
Close To me,
All you'll be
Fill Up my Heart
With your love

Is wandering more
How I'll see
With the eyes
You gave me
La La Ni Ni
It's more than a dream
When I stand before your face
It's his wonderment
I long to see
Bah Bah (Drums)

Miracles of Miracles   (LaLaLa LaLaLa, Dahhh Da Da)
He's standing here
Listening to my voices
As I draw near
To worship Him

(Fast Pace Angels Dance)
Halleluyahhhh
Halleluyahhhh
He Reigns
He Reigns
On High
He Reigns

God is good

HE SET ME FREE AUGUST 8, 2011

Open up the door
To terraces that never end
Leaving the pathways of light
For darkness
I'm bound
So Bound
Set me free
Open the doors
To where I want to be

Set me back on course
Before I drown
In the seas of death
Believing myself to be
Something stronger and you show me then
Nothing's alive until He saved us from sin
Angel are around you, assembled to help you, let go

Praise Hallelujah, thank you Father let me lay down my sin

IT'S TIME TO KNOW ME AUGUST 3, 2011

Some don't know how
So ashamed
Tell them to say
Lord I need your lovingkindness
To bridge the gap in my soul
I left the way of righteousness
And have forsaken the law of life.
I need your help.
I ask forgiveness for
All that I've done and
I pray to receive your grace.
In Jesus name, Amen.
Thank you Father.

Praise you God

WHEN I SEE YOU THEN YOU WILL BE BLESSED JULY 1, 2011

When I look at you I see
Doughnuts coffee on the windowsill
Things deeper noticing the way I feel
Truth jerked inside,
I know in you
There's realness and truth
I need to get back home

And shut the door
It's like when
I play a guitar chord
Just strumming-never playing at an end
Just listening
To different sins
Wanting to go in . . .
Home
Let the blood of Jesus cover me
(Angels are here-that's all you have to worry about)
Please me
Then you will see my glory manifest
I know what you have need of before you . . . ask

Glorify your name Father, Hallowed be thy name, Father thou art worthy of all praises forever and ever Amen.

I WANT YOU TO KNOW I LOVE YOU STILL CHILD
JULY 1, 2011

You want me alone with you
And I'm running
Lips are syncing in
I can't hear your voice
Listening to the others
Waiting on what you have to say
A reminder-I don't want the day
Something's missing
Something I don't want to do
There's no running
When I have to face you

You are so good
You are so good to me
Thank you Holy Father Alpha and Omega Amen

THE RESURRECTION AND LIFE AUGUST 8, 2011 (MOM'S BIRTHDAY)

The circumstances she was under
Was like a cloud by the Red Sea
She looked up to Heaven
And prayed
And I told her
She would see my Glory
Manifested to men
The Stone was rolled away
And I heard her cry
His body came out of the tomb
When I mentioned he wouldn't die
I heard her voice   La La La La LaLa La La Lay
Sound in the midst
Lord forgive me
When she saw him
And called
Lazarus
Lazarus I called
Lazarus
Lazarus I called
Lazarus
Lazarus I called
Lazarus
Lazarus I called
Lazarus
Lazarus I called
Lazarus
Lazarus I called
Lazarus
Then he awoken from his sleep
Angels around him
As others weep
Lazarus come forth!
The command I gave
Giving new life
To the man I saved

Worship your name Lord

YOU ARE EVERYTHING AUGUST 19, 2011

Father in Heaven
Forgive me
My sin is deep
Worshiping everything
When Angels call
And my mind sets straight
To hear the Father's will
When I want to be . . . next to you

So good to be close to you

YOU ARE AND ANSWER TO PRAYER AUGUST 10, 2011

A trillion stars in the sky
Effervescent, luminous
Appearing in the day
Behind a Sun so bright
Hidden in its' light
Peeking from beneath its' wondrous waves
Magnificent when the two are together
That's what Jesus does for me
I don't even have to think anymore
He leads me in the way of righteousness
Never a wondering heart
Always behind Him
Waiting for Him to intervene
In my circumstances
I don't feel the same anymore
The fear is gone
Nothing stands in the way
He has broken the barriers
Lead me to fields of Kindnesses
Giving to others
I haven't forgotten
The words you said
I need more of you Jesus

Your journey is different from others
You don't look behind you anymore
The lessons have taken awhile
However the end is in sight
Just worship me.

You're so good, that's all you want from me is to worship you, you're so good.

THE FATHER KNOWS MY NAME AUGUST 12, 2011

Astonished beyond measure
When she spoke to me
When Jesus saw her
He spoke to her
Woman where are thou accusers?
There aren't any
Neither do I condemn thee
Go and sin no more
Why should you look at my face?
Being so kind to me Lord?
I did nothing right
It was all by your righteousness.

I didn't see you fall
Oh woman of God
I saw your tears
As they here about to stone you
Waiting for rocks to hit you
Pleading with me to help you
You said, Oh Jesus if you can . . . please
And I heard your heart saying
Your blood shed for me
Then I stood and told them
If you have no sin cast the first stone
They walked away then
You where left there with me
Then I asked you
If you where accused
You surrendered to me then

Almighty God
I am ready
To seek your face
You erased all my pain
Took away the shame
Made me whole and new again
Why did I look away
When you gave love
Working pass the grave
I need you Lord
I can't let go now

Thank you Jesus

OH FATHER OF ALL THANK YOU LORD
AUGUST 12, 2011

Out of the intensity of sin
When I looked to you
Dirth and darkness all around
When you said
Emptiness be whole
Fill the skin
Leprosy depart
Nine went away
But I came back to say Thank you Lord
Thank you Lord
That's all He wanted them to say
For the miracle that day
That kept them in bondage all those years
With a destructive disease that ate their flesh
They wanted someone to hear their cries
And you heard them and healed them all
Why didn't they come back to say Thank you Lord
Why can't our hearts express what you need to hear
As often as we breathe
Just to say
Thank you Lord.

Thank you Lord
Thank you Lord

Oh Father, forgive me for not saying often as I spoke Thank you Jesus, Thank you Lord

WHEN I WANTED TO FIND AWAY OUT OF MY MESS AUGUST 14, 2011

A runaway slave
Finds his way home
It took a while for him to find
Where he belonged
Finding the north star again
Looking up in the woods
Asking, where are you?
Looking
Observing
Crying out
On bended knee
Until the light appeared
And he could move again
The trees had moss but he needed the light
Wishing His feet could move faster
Than they did at that moment
As desire tempted to overrun him
He had to push faster
They where chasing him
Like dogs panting
Desiring and seeking his soul
As his hands reached out
Saying, "Hold me Jesus"
The darkness around me
You're pulling me out of
Not just for myself
But for others
That don't see,
That are still in bondage,
For me to tell them

There is a way out
Waiting for the star to shine
Believing in God's gift to the earth
All glory to God
Amen

WHEN YOU WOKE ME AUGUST 16, 2011

You are like the
Leaves on the tree
That whisper in the wind
Come to me
Worship me
Talk to me
Don't forget what I've done for you
That I've given you life today
Let your eyes see me
Again

You measured my line again today God, thank you for using me and giving me life. You are the Almighty God.

LIKE THE SOUND OF A DEER PANTING FOR WATER AUGUST 16, 2011

Luscious grapes fall down from the vine
When deers walk under your branches
Crushing the grapes with their teeth
Looking about
For the danger lurking
Walking around them
They listen for the noise
Then scatter at a leaf branch sound
That comes to their ears
That a man has come in their midst
They wait and see
Behind hedges of green
Worshiping God
Hearts a beating

Faster rhythm
That's why we are trapped often in our thoughts
We don't see the hidden danger
Until it comes upon us
Worrying, thinking about tomorrow
Not realizing that He has given us life just for today
We left off understanding He knows our needs
We look pass what 's around us
To seeing what our hearts want to be
We forget
We are His kindness
That others should see
Whether in life or death
He is seen
Through our symphony of His love and
Our heart felt praise of His waking us His love

You are the answer to my prayers, you are the only one who loves me, I need you, thank you for today.
You've given me so much and I listen when you need me to be . . . your son.

LETTERS TO A LOVED ONE AUGUST 17, 2011

What's going on inside me
Why do I feel her heart today
Why am I tossing and turning
Crying out
Lord I need you
To give her grace in your sight
Let her see me
When you look at my heart
Let her see
What goes without saying
When she knows the lessons learned
Considering the lilies

Patiently waiting
I need you God

TAKING UP THE HURTING AUGUST 17, 2011

Capturing my soul
I can't look down anymore
At the trail of tears
I've left behind
When the cross comes near
Nothing more to stand on
Than a single whisper
"I know you my child"
"Walk with me"
Up the mountainside
Taking your cross
Giving me the burden
Taking another step
As there is an anointing
I want to give you
To reach out
And give them hope
In their darkest days
"I'm there"
Healing
Feeling
Kneeling before the Father
Asking the Father
For mercy

I know your needs before you ask

NEWNESS OF THE DAY AUGUST 20, 2011

Your Holy Spirit around me
So different
So beautiful
Like a shine from the glory of God
Something that makes you new
Totally unscathed
Clean
Holy

Innocent
Pure in heart
Kept by His mercy
That is unto us day by day
I wish I knew His presence like that
The Holiness of God

Thank you Father for another day

LETTING GO OF THE SIN AUGUST 21, 2011

Sinking below the waves
Trying to come up from below
When the current pushes away the surface
And the sea consumes my every movement
Stranded again
In a land of empty area
No one's around
I sleep in agony
Wishing I was able to talk
To Him . . . to Jesus
Maybe if I place everything at His feet
It could be different
Maybe joy

I need you

JESUS I NEED . . . . AUGUST 21, 2011

She sings when I don't hear
Her voice whispers
And I don't want her near
I push the door open
I walk away
She comes after me
Asking where I'm going
Touching me
Saying she loves me
Wanting me home again

And I hold her
Jesus I want to come back home
I don't want to stay away
Can't hear the birds
Can't hear when you say
Those nice things to me

Your voice is so kind

THE JESUS SONG AUGUST 15, 2011

Could you not wait up one hour for me   La La LaLaLa
                                             Lah Lah Lahh La Lah

When you slept there I was by the tree
Praying that you have life through me

Could you not wait up one hour for me

It mattered as I shed my blood
From my head for thee

Could you not wait up one hour for me

See how I knelt
Before Calvary

Could you not wait up one hour for me

As the angels knelt
And comforted me

Could you not wait up one hour for me

Caused by God's love
To set you free

Could you not wait up one hour for me

I know you where tired

Resting well

Could you not wait up one hour for me

When I woke you, you thought I had a story to tell
But I wanted you to know, it was coming

Could you not wait up one hour for me

When I would be tossed over for the world to see
How much I loved thee (trails in the end)

(Quietly)
Could you not wait up one hour for me
Could you not wait up one hour for me
Could you not wait up one hour for me

I need to wait

HE TOOK AWAY MY SHAME AUGUST 21, 2011

Jesus you took me from within myself
Destructive tendencies all that was left
Noises in my head
Wouldn't leave me alone
Demons
Being led
Then Jesus spoke
And they went away
The people, the Master
What a scene
Nobody moved
When the pigs ran down
Into the sea
All that was left was Jesus and me
I felt His arms
I didn't want to leave
You have to tell others
He told me

And then I walked and went back home
Telling them about the Lord who saved me
Wondering how I can tell them He loves me

When I look around He's near

HE'S HERE WITH ME AUGUST 23, 2011

He's with me
He's my surging strength
The answer to my call
When foundations crumble
He will stand

Thank you God for being my all

YOU ARE THE HOLY ONE OF ISRAEL AUGUST 24, 2011

Angels walking down the steps
With presents for His people
Wind chimes blowing in the wind
Eclipsing the shattered dreams
Walking, pacing
Listening to their Master's will
When He speaks a heavenly chord
"If you will love me
I'll teach you new things"
Fountains are rising

They are worshiping me
Touching wing to wing
Shouting
Holy is the Lord our God
Who is, who was, who is to come
He is the Almighty God
The angels glimmer
As they worship the Lord pure and holy and true
Wings unfurled

Shimmering in the light of day
Their expanse stretches over the heavens
As they call out to you
"To Him that is Holy
Be mercy and grace"
I feel my fingers rising
As I praise thee
Archangels do the Master's will
At His command
Hearing His voice
As they bow down
Before thee
The darkness bends at His will
A calmness resides in my soul
There is a dampening of evil's hold
A re-commitment to His Holy way
The effects of His love on my soul

Thank you Lord for this poem an expression of your love to me

WHEN HE SEEKS ME OUT IN THE MORNING LIGHT AUGUST 24, 2011

The bows of arrows bend
Shooting straight up in the sky
Rising higher
Falling back to earth
So is my love for thee

Worship you Lord Jesus

WHEN THE LORD HEARS MY VOICE AUGUST 24, 2011

Lord purify my heart
Worship me
Then you will see my fire
Consuming
Everything that needs purging

Like water coming springing up
The earth cleansing the natural substances away
Emitting
Words of life
When you cleanse
And your arms spread before me
Inclining
To learn my ways
And be filled with His Righteousness
Who sits on the throne
By the blood of the Lamb
Washing us whole and new

Make me more like you

WHEN YOU SAW ME LAYING THERE
AUGUST 25, 2011

Parenthetical observations
Connecting the lies within me
Considering my circumstances
Seeking your face
A hurricane's in the distance
Shoulders bulging
Exerting pressure
Holding back
The storm within me
Boundaries unsettled
A constant flux
Severing ties
Concluding the matter
You called to me
When you saw me rolling in the dust
Saying "Here my child"
Wash away the tear
The agony
Hard to come back?
I hear you . . . come.

Let me listen to your voice once again

I GAVE YOU A NEW SONG TO SING WITH THE ANGELS AUGUST 25, 2011

Collusion of elements
Create a new song
That enters the palace
Of His praises
Where angels dwell
Keeping Him in worship
Like
Bomp Bomp Da Da Da
We praise you lord
We praise you Lord
God Almighty
Hallowed be they name
Thy Kingdom come
Thy will be done
On Earth
As it is in Heaven
And we praise you this day
As you give us our daily bread

And Lead us not into temptations
As we forgive those who trespass against us
Keep us from evil
For thine is the kingdom Da da DaDaDa
And the Power
And the glory
Forever (Forrr . . . evvvv . . . errrrr)

You are so good Holy Spirit Holy is your name. Thank you for allowing me to enter into worship with you Father

WHEN THE DAWN SEEMS SO FAR AWAY AUGUST 26, 2011

On the cross
The reservoir of your heart muscle
Overflowing
To bring me everything I need

Muscles relax
Strength coming back in His body
As He says the last words,
For me.
Heart heavy
It will be broken
God will put it back together
For us to sing to Him again
So we can smile
And tell God He is our all

Nothing left inside us.

But to believe

To give you everything

HIDE ME IN YOUR PAVILION AUGUST 26, 2011

A secret place
I need to be beside you
Out of the storm and the mist
Hidden alone to worship you
Encouraged by your heart's cry
To worship you and cry out for the soul's of men
Humbly
Waiting and listening
For your directions
To come again to the place
Where you can bring the song
And whisper in my ear
What you need me to hear

Don't hold back God

JESUS KNOWS OUR EVERY WEAKNESS
AUGUST 26, 2011

I just couldn't pray today
I didn't have the words to say
I know He wants to hear me
But it didn't happen that way
I couldn't get them to come
The words faltered
They wouldn't list
I couldn't tell Him the idea
Everything seem to miss
I don't know how to pray to you
So I'll just open my heart
And say the first word on my lips
Jesus I adore you
And hope you'll
Enjoy it

Thank you Father,

CALLING OUT TO YOU AUGUST 29, 2011

Thank you God
For another day
Thank you for waking me
And for the things I say
Everyday is different
From where I stand
No day like it as it begins again
Looking to Jesus
Worshiping Him again
Looking away from the filth and the sin
Getting the newness looking to end
The things in my mind that waste away
Refuse and lies things I don't want to say

I need you

Happy day

WHEN THERE ARE NO WORDS TO SAY
AUGUST 30, 2011

It's like when he calmly walks after me
People talking, everybody's whispering
And He puts His hand over me
I feel safe
They have left me alone
They have walked away
She's standing against the wall
Waiting for His love

Lonely alone waiting for His call
When others matter when others fall
Dangers ahead I know them well
Working behind the bars
Letting others dwell
While I suffered

He listened
Then called after me
Holy and pure
I want thee to be
Amen. Thank you Lord Jesus.

SOME TIMES YOU CAN'T DO IT BY YOURSELF
AUGUST 31, 2011

You bring laughter to me
I'm no more that man that looked around
Wondering who was at his back
Thoughts of redemption
That was what I lacked
I never looked at what would happen to me
A desperate attempt when I'm underneath
Considering the changes dragging my feet

Another callous attempt at having it my way
When nothing's left, nothing to say
Worn out excuses that leave me empty
Unclean experiences in infrequent places
Certain that no one saw me enjoy the tastes
Of mind blowing drugs that leave traces
Of my inadequacies
Personal vendettas
Left in the inner spaces
Considering the drama
That surfaces in my mind
Blue skies fall away
Let me be
Humbly I bow down and seek
To turn the tide
Shadows of darkness
You can no more abide
In His love

Jesus, I need to welcome you in

FATHER KNOWS BEST SEPTEMBER 1, 2011

Worship your name Lord
Wings that bow
Angels in the midst
Wondering
Why I wake so late
When praises return to Him early
By mouths of many
Standing with hearts blazing
Praying that he will hear
Begging for mercies
Waiting to hear an answer that
Provides peace in their hearts
So that others can be set free

Thank you Father

I'M CALLING TO YOU WILL YOU HEAR MY VOICE
SEPTEMBER 1, 2011

Cavern
Deep streams with in me
Darkness abode
Ravines not passable
Inherent thought trains
Loosening my inner gorge
Rhythmic heartbeats
Longing to refrain
From being kidnapped
By evil's way

Jesus stands on the other side
Come to me
And I want to
My heart is divided
Watching
Looking for a way
To get across to you
And the light of your love shows
How well a bridge was constructed
In the cavernous region
To cleanse me

Just like Jesus
Just when I called
Looking to the right and the left
Then taking the first step
Toward the home in your heart
Nobody notice my tears in the back
As I walked forward
Desiring what I lacked
Nothing to hold me back
Nothing to care
Wouldn't quite call it
The struggle ending

But I didn't care
I know it's a journey
That struggles persist
Any while longer I will miss
Encouraged by the sacrifice on the cross
He without speaking saying anything remiss
Just looking at them with pain
As He said Father forgive them
They know not the shame
Of what they are doing
They worry about themselves
What they will buy
With the clothes I had
While looking at the dice
I see their faces
Tragically unconcerned
While I pay
The penalty for man
Seeking their own way
Living large
Wondering what their next move will be
Clueless about the man on the tree
Who lives forevermore
While they pour another flask into their mouth
To forget the pain,
They can't escape
Warring, which seems to consume their being
Never leaving the fields of blood
Consume by their passions and lusts to forget
When all they need to do is turn to me
And listen to my voice
Not caring what others think
Angels in the midst now
I'm about to leave
It is finished
Darkness falls
Now they see
"This was the Son of God!"

All who hear it let them bow down before Him,
Jesus you are my all, I hunger for thee,
You alone gave your love for me
On the tree

Amen, God you are wonderful and loving to me
Amazing to me
Thank you Jesus . . . Amen

Amen

HIS GLORY IS EVIDENT THROUGHOUT ALL CREATION 9/1/2011

Glorious   (clap, clap)   LaLaLa La La Lah La La
Glorious   (clap, clap)
Glorious unto the Lamb . . . we sing
Glorious   (clap, clap)
Glorious   (clap, clap)
Glorious to the Lamb . . . we . . . sing   LaLaLa La La Lah La . . . La . . .
Glorious   "   "
Glorious   "   "
Glorious unto the King of Kings
Glorious   "   "
Glorious   "   "
Glorious to the Lamb . . . we . . . sing
Glorious   "   "
Glorious   "   "
Glorious to the King of Kings
Glorious   "   "
Glorious   "   "
Glorious to the Lamb . . . we . . . sing

Halleluyah   "   "
Halleluyah   "   "
Halleluyah praise the Lord
Halleluyah   "   "
Halleluyah   "   "

Halleluyah praise . . . the . . . Lord
Halleluyah   "   "
Halleluyah   "   "
Jesus you are wonderful
Halleluyah   "   "
Halleluyah   "   "
Jesus you . . . are . . . wonderful
Praise . . . . the . . . Lord . . . . (last line of last staza)

(Song to be sung in churches across the world).

YOU ARE HOLY MOST RIGHTEOUS GOD
SEPTEMBER 1, 2011

(They-the angels-quietly)

Glory in the highest
Holy One of Israel
You are so wonderful
Your name is Holy
The angels sing
Immersed in your glory
As we sing
Holy, Holy, Holy,
Now we look at your face
And kneel our wings in thy perfect place
Amen.

FATHER YOU ARE AWESOME SEPTEMBER 1, 2011

La La La La La La Lah . . . . Lah

Your glory is so awesome
Your glory is so awesome
Like a minion in the ocean
Is my love to thee.

Your glory is so awesome
Your glory is so awesome

Open my eyes in the morning
Is all that I can see

Your glory is so awesome
Your glory is so awesome
I worship thee,
Purchased by His blood, died upon the tree

Your glory is so awesome
Your glory is so awesome
We are washed cleaned by His blood
As He was nailed horribly to a piece of wood

Father-thy name is holy
Holy awesome and mighty
To awesome to even speak
Your Holy Majesty
We worship thee

Halleluyah, we sing
We sing,
Almighty God, Lord of love, Amen.

YOUR HANDS SWIFT TO SHED INNOCENT BLOOD
SEPTEMBER 2, 2011

Terrible sin they said
Watching her wake laying in the bed
He slept beside her but they didn't care
It was her they wanted to take her to the Master's care
They took her there
Standing in front of Him
What do you say Rabbi
As He scooped sand on the ground
Refusing to look at them
And what they found
Listening instead to the voice of His dad
Who told Him to let them know

How to give mercy and grace and
Warn her as He let her go
They waited again then He looked at them
Slowly rising telling themselves
If you are without sin cast the first stone
In a sense otherwise leave her alone
They looked at themselves filled with their sin
And then began
To drop their rocks, first the old then the young men
They went away understanding in their hearts
That He had said something that imparted love
It left them unsure
When He looked in their eyes and said those words
Removing self-righteousness, how great we think we are
Letting us see, what's really in our hearts
Something we won't look at until he makes us see
I made you, I didn't make your hatred of others
You can't say you love me
And not love your brother
I see and hear the things you said
Listening to your heart
That comes up to me daily
I know the sin that fills your mind
The thoughts that gather
When your mind's at ease
Thinking of things that might please
Your mind and body, fleshly wants
That don't care about others
Considering the sin
Travesty of the mind that's certainly bent
Towards all kinds of evil despising the love
Toward another
Letting them go of their sin
He told her Sin no more

Thank you Lord I needed that, to stay on track
I needed you to intervene in my situation
Letting me know your heart, getting right with you

Telling others you are special, doesn't matter the cost
Doesn't matter the cost
Jesus knows our every weakness take it to the Lord in prayer

A gentle wind breezes through lovingkindness
A course wind throws our hearts and binds us
Holiness is not concerned about who gets what
It's only measure is where our hearts are aligned with His grace?

You are driving the car Jesus

THERE IS A WAY THAT SEEMS RIGHT TO A MAN THE END THEREOF IS DEATH 9/4/11

I feel your love for me
It comes from an answer to prayer
From God alone
No one else can do it
Makes me seem whole and new again
I've left that life, left it alone
I don't want to go back to it
He brings me joy
He brings me life
My heart is open
To love Him more
Than any time before

Your love is so strong to me, so good to me, why do you love me. He's so good
to me.

FATHER YOU ARE GLORIOUS 9/4/11

Angels around you Lord
Let your name be praised
And all blessings come up to you
Bless today Father
Let us bless your name
High in the Midst of heaven
Glorify your name

Holy, holy, Holy
Glorify your name
Praise your name
Wonderful One
Counselor
Majesty on High
We worship you
When angels sing
Glory
The whole earth shakes
And knees will bow to thee
Grant us grace and mercy
In Jesus Christ Holy Name
Amen

WHEN HE REACHES DOWN TO ME 9/5/2011

He Prince of Peace is here to help you
Stop what you're doing and
Hear His voice
In the still quiet
Listen
Be still
And know I Am God

Thank you Father

A SONG FROM THE HEAVENLY PLACE 9/5/11

Bee dee op tha tha tha

The Lion's waiting
For those who will share
In the banquet feast
That is prepared for by
The angels of heavenly grace
Singing and dancing and playing
This song
What a friend we have in Jesus

All our sins and griefs to bare
What a privilege to carry
Everything to God in prayer
Would we find a friend so faithful
Who will all our sorrows share
Jesus knows our every weakness
Take it to the Lord in prayer.

Thank you God

THANK YOU JESUS FOR MY WIFE TO BE
SEPTEMBER 6, 2011

An offering comes up out of her soul
She is playing to her Master
With her lips on the flute
Letting Him know she loves Him
Speaking His words
She worships with her heart
Letting her lungs fill
To exhale a breathe of love telling others
He is the one who loves me more than the Red Sea
Certainly she wields powerfully
The whispers of airy grace
That call out to me
She listens to the words I say
Even when they are loud
And gently
Lowers her voice
Touching me
Telling me It's going to be okay
And I listen
When we hold
I say "I love you"
"I love you too"
Jesus I love you
She's amazing

Why do I deserve your goodness and mercy such evident grace? You are so good to me. You are Lord,
I bow down before thee. Worship thee.
Make me three lanterns one gold, another ginger and the last a diamond, this is what you will give her on her birthday
Then she'll give her love to thee
Freely
This is why God loves thee
Angels are singing in Heaven
That she's waiting for thee
A woman of God's love
That He's given to thee
Amen.

SORROW ENDURES FOR A NIGHT
SEPTEMBER 11, 2011

We were there
The planes hit
We didn't understand
You saw us
You heard us
We repented
Your hand
Gave us new life

Oh Father you are so good to us, we don't deserve your mercy but thank you.

WHEN I SPEAK SEPTEMBER 13, 20011

Scientists receive
But they don't understand
Innumerable phrases
A deepening hand
Social regimes tortures of the past
Society' calling-the promise land
There is a distance between us
Without His hope
Bridged by His love

When we had no hope
Curious answers written out before us
Man's inability to reach out before us
To touch Him

You are so wonderful to me, Thank you for allowing me back your His presence

WHY DO YOU ASK? SEPTEMBER 13, 2011

Five billion songs he gives to people every day
Some understand some go their way
He wakes them during the day
And speaks to their heart
It pays to listen
To believe in Him

Then when they sing
We listen

The Holy Spirit gives them
Thank you Lord

GOD IS WITH ME SEPTEMBER 14, 2011

Come before His Throne
With thanksgiving and singing

Come before His Throne
With thanksgiving and singing

Da Da Dah Dah Dah
Dah Dahhhh-Da Dot dot

(Tapping His foot on the Throne
Every creature flying by-praising Him)

Glorify His name
Before His Holy Face

Glorify His name
Before His Holy Face
Dance with joy
Before His Holy Face

Dance with joy
Before His Holy Face

(Sing aloud
Sing aloud)

Part 2 of song Trumpets Up, Note high

"Praise !!!!"

Dance with joy (Little faster)
(In circle all around revolution
Singing dancing all, Up and Down
Twirl-Worship

(THIS TO BE A MUSICAL CALLED **WORSHIP HIM**)

Glorify thy name
Glorify thy name
Glorify thy name
In all the earth

(This song (sung) in the midst of
Dance (Dancing with Joy) As all
Around music celebration

Thank you Father for this song from heaven

THERE IS A FOUNTAIN WIDE AND DEEP 9/15/11

Freed me from my chains of self doubt
Working out
The self-abasement issues
Until you were so real to me

Never looking back
At the home I prepared
To tarry there
Where
He had never seen me to be
Never wanted me to be
Gave His love to me
Brought me back from the brink
Standing over the sink
Mom called
Just as I moved to end it all
The darkness and the gloom scattered then
When the doorbell rang and they entered in
His hand was upon me then
"No my child, I need you,"
For what you'll do for me

You were there God when I needed you most-surrounding me,
A garment of praise for the spirit of heaviness

I HEARD HER VOICE 9/15/11

When she cried out I heard her voice
When I looked at her knowing
Her sin
I came to her
Daughter
You who once sinned
Are cleansed
Rise now
Be my Jewel to go all over the world
That they may know me
Yes, Jesus

You worship me, so I put my life inside you

FACING THE GIANT 9/15/11

It's a hole we feel we're without
Missing something
So we drive our brains in vain
Thinking about the past failures
We drive ourselves insane
Saying there is no way out
When there is always hope in Jesus
The negative takes place
We don't hear His promises,
Straining our ears at the voices
Letting the enemy come in
Doubt, disappointment and dispair
And we must rebuke them
Or we feel closed off
The pains of loneliness
When He is still there
Our brothers and sisters are there
He sends His word to uplift us
The brokenness we feel
He scatters the illusion
Remembering all that He can do

You are mine child, I needed you to see, so that others might see, Me.

WHEN WE KNEEL AT HIS FEET 9/15/11

Broken vessel
Nothing more
All poured out
Empty inside
Drained
Then you can use me
Nothing left
A seed of belief
Instructional
Now you can come to me
I can use you

Before you were
Bringing you
While I waited
And let
Until you were cleaned
Now I'll use you
Now
Amen

IN HEAVEN THEY ARE HAPPY 9/15/11

(A praising song, like dancing angels)
LaLa La LaLa
(Starts off)
How are you doing
Up in the kingdom   La da da da da
Their finding out the source of strength-is Jesus   La da da da da

They're worshiping him   Ka boom Da Da Da Da Da
Around the throne

Having their robes
Washed in His blood

Worshiping Him
On their knees before Him

Walking Down
The Streets of Gold

La da   da   da da   Ka boom
La da   da   da da   Ka boom
La da   da   da da

Angels are walking
To and fro

There is so much joy and happiness in Heaven, oh Lord you are so good to give worship songs.

WHEN YOU LOOK AT THE CROSS
SEPTEMBER 18, 2011

Chastised for our peace
Left alone for our sin
As the sun burned Him
Bearing our sin and shame
His goodness spread over me

Thank you Father for all you have given to me

THERE IS A NEW SONG IN MY HEART
SEPTEMBER 20, 2011

The human heart morphs
At the thought of loving you
Watching the angels bow
Their wings unfurled
Standing in your presence
Below your grace
Seeking to know you more
Waiting for your introspection
We wait
There is a call to our hearts
To be like you
But cancerous tissues
Keep us from connecting
And we call out to you
Oh Great Physician
And your scalpel of love
Cuts away the diatrious
Dissolving the issues
That made us mortified
To be in your presence

It is well with my soul now
Thank you Jesus
Thank you
Amen

I WANT TO SHOW YOU MY GOODNESS
SEPTEMBER 21, 2011

Take no thought for me
I am here for thee
Though you don't know me
Nor who I am
I am concerned about thee

So ask me about tomorrow
While today is still
Whisper in my ear
What you want this year
Tell me what's inside
Then my hands shall . . .
Move
Over you (Overrrrrr Youuuuuu)
La La La La

YOU ARE ALL I NEED SEPTEMBER 23, 2011

I feel your presence around me
Your power surges through me
Like a cord wire
Taken by surprise
I realize
That all I am in you
Began
As I set my feet to follow you
Then found myself where I didn't want to be
Stuck
And I couldn't get out of my darkness
Waiting for relief
Then you told me
Just wait on me
I'm listening
I heard you the other night,
While you were in bed

Touching you
Telling you
I'm here

*I love you Jesus, thank you for telling me you were there and are here with me.
When you are near I feel good.*

Amen

LET ME FEEL YOUR LOVE TO ME, GOD YOU ARE NEAR SEPTEMBER 24, 2011

Anointing of grace fall on me now
Cleansing me
As I worship you
A stirring in my soul
Jesus you are here
A deepening grace
You called me
I woke up
I hear your voice
Coming near

O glorify your name
Thank you Lord
Oh Glory, Glory
To your name
Angels are around me
I am blessed
You are God
You are so good to me
Peace flows through me
And over me
And I am new inside
Desiring to please you
To love again
Give them grace
I just worship you

Your glory come into this place
Make us all new

Majesty on High

Wonderful One

GUILTY STAINS WASHED AWAY SEPTEMBER 24, 2011

Bless your name
Bless your name Lord
Bless your holy Spirit
Worshiping Blanket of praise
Praise to your name
Holy, Holy, Holy
You are the most righteous EL
The God of Jacob
There is none like you
I kneel
Oh God let our souls rejoice in you
Worship your name
Exalt thee
Exalt you
Praise you Yahweh
You are the light of our lives
The eternal One
Who sings to me daily
Worship Thee
Oh Mighty One

You are righteous and holy now
Let's be cleansed

Thank you Father

I CONSIDER THE CROSS SEPTEMBER 25, 2011

Nevertheless as winter comes
I will seek your home above
Reaching out to you
In the harsh rains of life
That water my soul
Your calming hand
Steadies me
Soft wind of Heaven
Blow over my soul
Listen as I sing to thee
Worship, praise

THE POWER OF HIS RESSURECTION
SEPTEMBER 25, 2011

Partly open
Partly closed
The tomb
Opening for Him
The King of Glory
Death could not hold Him
Hell and the grave lost their touch
As He took the keys
Away
Opening the graves
Letting the saints go
The soldiers fell away
His eyes
The empty tomb
Stone rolled away
The power of God revealed
Resurrecting the dead
Into the city
The saints trod
As they watched
Mouths opened

The weapons of our warfare are not carnal
But mighty through God to the pulling
Down of strongholds

So why do we fear?

IT'S A CALL TO YOUR HEART SEPTEMBER 25, 2011

The glory of God is here
All you have to do is reach out and touch it
It's available to you
Consuming you
Want it?
It's waiting
Why are you resistant
Can't you hear my voice calling?
I want to be (leave the life of sin) with you
In you shining like a light
That brings the light dissolving the dark night
Of the nations
They need Me (in you) now
They are dying
Don't wait to long

FIRE IS GONE OUT SEPTEMBER 25, 2011

The springs of water
Fall down to the earth from your heart
That branches
Into rivers
Gulleys
Sanctuary you need
To contain the flow
From His heart
You can't hear
The overflow of my love for you
Because there have been imaginations
Contending with my love for you
Broken dreams of the past

Keeping you locked down
Subduing your witness
Till the fire lightens gently
Satisfied with a flicker
When I want you to burn brightly with me
No more contained
Stages of development completed
Ready to war against the enemy
With no hesitation
For me

Fire of God burn in me, (make me whole and new, take me where I need to be)

SECOND CORINTHIANS 4:17 OUR LIGHT AFFLICTIONS . . . . SEPT 25, 2011

Holiness to the Lamb
Holiness unto Jesus
Scratching the surface of my pain
Eternal suffering again and again
Leads me to the cross
Like never before
Bowing on my knees
Knowing I can't ignore
His . . . love

WHEN SHE SOFTLY COMES BEFORE ME SEPTEMBER 27, 2011

She wakes up saying Jesus I love you
There is a snippet of grace about her
She humbly comes before me
Worshiping
Her heart is like glass
Truthfulness is in her voice
When she explains the situations
And listens to my words of help
She breathes
And tells me the truth

Laying her soul bare in my presence
Looking up to me with untoward eyes
Her eyes sing to me
And I hear her voice
A struggle in her heart
I'll bring her out of it
She's got an angel around her
Telling her-it's going to be okay

HIS KINDNESS EXTENDED TO ME SEPTEMBER 27, 2011

Falsetto voice
In woods behind
Unhinged phrases
Deciphering lines
Of the Spirit's
Love for me
That's what I hear
In her voice

Thank you Father

WHEN I PRAISE HIM, HE LET'S ME KNOW WHAT THE ANGELS ARE SINGING 9/27/11

(Rhythm of song)
Boom Boom
Tikel
Boom Boom
(Continuously)

A Glorious day
Was made by the Father

In His love for me
It's not a matter of what I want to be

Shadows of the grave
That wash over me

He has removed
Giving life to me

A Lion roars
With a distant cry

Verdant colors
Of His royal majesty

The Lord is gracious

For all to see

Waking up reading

His word to me.

Thank you Father

WHEN YOU WALK DOWN THE PATHWAYS SEPTEMBER 28, 2011

When you walk down the path ways
The answer comes
Letting you know
Why I showed you what was happening
I hear you calling me
Stripes ran down my back
Unifying the saints
Anointed power of God falls in places
Satan's uses are broken
And people live again
To worship you Lord

YOU MADE ME HAPPY SEPTEMBER 28, 2011

I saw you praising me the other day
Listening to my voice
And I wanted to share with you
That you are walking in my steps
It makes me happy to see you
Considering my love for you
That I am in the midst
My God is going to tare down the works of the enemy
And the angels of God shall move on my behalf
To minister to the nations
And His glory shall fall on
The dark places bringing light
Only let me praise Him more

God is so good to me

WHEN I FALL DOWN HE PICKS ME UP SEPTEMBER 28, 2011 ROSH

My heart is open to receive your love
Cascading into my heart
Exploding inside me
God gives his immeasurable grace to me
Her womb was dead inside
They laughed at Samuel's mother
Then she prayed
God heard her voice
And her son was given over to Him
Just like Jesus was given over
Fiery serpents burnt around Moses feet
But the sign of the cross made them flee
I'm building something new in you

HE HELD MY HAND OCTOBER 2, 2011

Sloughing through the mire
Understanding where I left off
Someone said it was when I left His face
Scared afraid of the day before
When He called my name
Peter
You will deny me three times
It seemed irrelevant
It couldn't be so
And then I said it
His face looked at me
Then I turned and walked through the door
The tears were hot
As they streamed down my face
I couldn't stop them
No matter how hard I tried to erase
What I had done
He found me sometime later
When he whispered do you love me
And I felt the tears again
When He told me
And I answered three times
Restoring me
I had looked away
He found me where I was at
Saying "I forgive you"
Never the same
Now I love Him more

WHY DID YOU GO TO THE CROSS FOR ME?

The opening in her heart is like
A fountain of joy
As she sings unto you Lord
The guilty stains you wash away
Then the crowd parts

She is alone with you
You turn to her
Are there none that accuse you
Not one Lord
Neither I condemn thee, go and sin no more
He takes her hand and lifts her up
Her eyes well up with tears
Jesus I love you her heart says
He touches her hair
She puts her face in His hand
Peace exudes from His hand to her face
A tear flows down her cheek

At the cross she looks at Him again
Is he the one that touched my cheek
Why are they cursing at Him?
He's done nothing wrong
Oh Jesus if I could take your place
Wipe the blood away from your face
Comfort you as you comforted me
Jesus I love you

<u>SUCH A GOD OCTOBER 5, 2011</u>

Hung There
Bleeding and dying
The weight of the world
Blood running
Feet hurting pushed
Mouth open praying

Thieves beside Him crying out
One wanting to be free of the pain of life
The other wanting to be free of the pain of sin
He listened to both
Only one heard His voice
Today you will be with me in paradise

Forgiven and
Clean
Never to wonder again
If I am saved
The look on His face of mercy
In so much pain

Tolerating
The jeers
The thirst
Vinegar they gave the King of Kings
For me

Talking to His Father
In the midst of
Pain and suffering
Leaving no doubt
That all was accomplished and finished
Then he bowed His head and gave up His spirit

I shed tears then
So much love
Incomprehensible
That He should die for me
Vile that I am
Such a God

HE SAVED A WRETCH LIKE ME OCTOBER 5, 2011

He lives
The grave is empty
Death defeated
Hell had no hold
The grave left empty-handed

I left that day
Feeling relief
That it was over
A roman soldier

Who had seen it all that day
The rain
Something about it
Truly this man was the Son of God
What have we done?
He was . . . .
God forgive us what we have done
I didn't know
When he spoke to the Father
I listened to the thieves
Ignoring their pleas
And gave Jesus a drink
I should not have put the crown on His head
Watching the cranial blood as it ran red
Watching them pull His beard
Putting the nails in His hands
I saw He was in pain
But I made sport
With the whip with metal chards
I treated Him disdainfully

He did nothing wrong to me
As I heard Him once say
Father forgive them for they know not what they do . . .
I died that day
Nothing left within me
I grasp a bottle of bitters later that day to forget
The pain came back
When He said it is finished
I became scared
The clouds and rocks moved
The shapes going back into the city from the grave
The veil rent looking into the Holy of Holies
As the rain beat me for my injustice
I was late
They made me go back out and guard the tomb
The seal upon it
Lightning . . . an angel
We fell as dead men
Running to the city

We tried to tell them
They paid us to lie
I wasn't the same
Set there for a day
Then went back the third day
A woman was there-talking to angels
Then to the gardener-it was Him
He is Risen
She told them
And I couldn't conceive
So I sat there
Two from Emmaus came and said they saw Him
I heard it and climbed up a ladder to look within
Then he appeared
The nail prints where in His hand
How?
I am the resurrection and the life
What have I done?
I need you
Jesus, please come and save a wretch like me

LIKE A LITTLE LAMB LOST OCTOBER 7, 2011

Heal me
I went into sin
I don't know why
It didn't appeal to me
But I need to get back in your presence
My mind goes back to where
It doesn't want to be
I say things I don't want to say
When you look at me
My heart aches to be near
Where I once wanted to be
Like a lamb that has gone its' own way
Tired and distance
Not observing
How far I've gone
Until you come looking for me

THAT OTHERS MAY SEE ME OCTOBER 7, 2011

Forgive me Jesus
Rescue my soul
Set me free
To be the bird I use to be
Wings outstretched
Nothing hindering me

Cleanliness in worship
No more need to worry
Bow down and worship Him
Let Him hear your voice
Clean me in worship
Make me new again
Let your words hit my soul like a hammer
Renewed faith
That others may believe

Darkness shall depart
The angels shall come in
You can come back in
Then the angels will move about you
And you'll hear my voice
Telling you to kneel
And worship me

Thank you Father, thank you Lord

GO ON OCTOBER 7, 2011

Get inside your head
Thoughts abound
That don't need to be
You have the answer
Forgive

A heart goes on beating
In the distant wind
Saying Lord please
Use me again
I don't know what to say
How I got this way
I don't want to remain
I have to be different

You are my child
I see you as a Prince and Princess
I've covered your sin
Now go out
And praise me
Worship the one that made you
And gave you eternal life
You are not to be here settling
But on the front lines
No more doubt or disappointment
I've freed you from sin
While you are here
They are waiting
Go

IT CAME UPON A MIDNIGHT CLEAR
OCTOBER 8, 2011

Feelings of God
Like torrents in the sea
I feel them in the wind
The music surrounds me
And I want to lift my head
And worship you
And let all the rains wash away
The darkness in my heart
The symphony that took away my joy
It's in Jesus
I'm ready

To take my place again
Exalting his name
Stars will fall all around me
But I will rise to arms lifted to praise thee
In indomitable praise
Worshiping
Let the church doors open

Thank you Father

DON'T LET ME GO OCTOBER 8, 2011

Sometimes I feel alone
When storms rise
Your hand slips away
I don't know where to look
It's scary
You were there before
I didn't worry
Now I see blackness

You meet my needs
When you come and save me
I need you closer
Hold me
Keep me safe

And I will always love you Jesus

NOTHING LEFT OCTOBER 8, 2011

The Fire of God is going out
Nothing Left to show
The Presence has left
Desert is forming
Dry and dampened
Buzzards and ravens
Stacked against the sky
Listening to the labored breathing

The death rattle
Nothing left to give
Dry as a willows oak
Burning out

Seeds need to be planted
For more growth
Fairest Lord Jesus
Ruler of all nature
Heal me

YOU MAKE ME BOW DOWN TO YOU
OCTOBER 8, 2011

Listen to the cry of
The Englishman
Gallantry displayed
When He falls

Sovereign Lord
The day grows dark
Praise you
That will restore me

WALKING DOWN THE STREET WITH JESUS
OCTOBER 9, 2011

She walks down the waves
Her hand stretches out in the wind
Her name warm in the sunshine
Her hair glistens
I want to feel her face
I know her by name
She is my child
When she went to bed I was there
Her feet were cold and I covered them
Her bible open by the candlelight
She reads my word early in the morning

I hear her voice
When she sounds like her world is ending
And I surround her with guardians and sentinels, her angels
She walks crying openly
About a relationship failed
I touch her arm
And tell her I love you

When her parents are gone
I will be there
Walking on the waves
Where her children play
Looking at her laughing
Enjoying life with play

Then I'll take her hand at the end of time
Saying I'm here in heaven-come
Then she'll rise up to me
Breaking through the clouds
Pass the sun and moon
Into my throne room
Where I'll say child welcome

She's been my daughter
Since the day she was born
I put in her sweetness
That others might see
Her grace
And blessed her
That others might see me
Through the smiles and laughter
When I lighten her face

I AM the Lord

HE HAS HANDS THAT HEAL OCTOBER 11, 2009

Healer
Putting things back together as they were
I can't began to say thank you
When nothing felt right
No one knew
You knew what I needed
Like Solomon crying out to thee
Saying I don't know what to do
To rule
And prayed for wisdom
You gave him more than he could believe

Your hands put my heart back together
After the pain
When she left me
And I fell to my knees
Crying out to you
To take away the pain
And you brought relief
Shored me up again

In my unworthiness I couldn't see
The enemy was sent to destroy me
But you gave me hope
And renewed my life again
When I let go of the anger, let go of the sin
And repented

Heal me O Lord
Heal me O God

Thank you Father

WHEN MUSIC FEEDS MY SOUL OCTOBER 11, 2011

Praise you thank you Lord Jesus
Thank you Father of all
You are so Holy
There is none like you
You are the Mighty One
There is no other name above Your Name
You are Righteous
I don't deserve to be around thee
Thou art Holy
I am a groundhog
Before your face

Holy, holy Holy
Is your name
Merciful and Mighty are your Grace
You are Holy
Worship you Oh Holy Father
Exalt thy name in the Heavens
Let the peoples praise thee
And give all honor and glory to thee

Thou art worthy
To receive Honor and Glory
At they footstep
We bow down
You are Worthy to be praised
With our hearts
We worship thee

Angels worship thee
In orderly rows
Saying Holy, Holy, Holy
Your glory beholds them
They wait upon thee
Now stand before me, my son

You are so Holy
Angels are all around you
Millions singing
Worship the Lamb of God
They walk around singing,
As He blesses everyone
They are without number
He knows them by name
When He calls they appear
Before Him
Without wrinkle
They wait upon Him
To serve Him

Thank you for the healing God
You are Righteous and Holy
You made all things to be
You are the life
I fear thee Oh Lord
Maker of Heaven and Earth

ENTERING IN WITH PRAISES OCTOBER 13, 2011

That our tears might fall to the ground
As we worship you
Feeling the fire come down
Letting the burn take us through
As we reminisce in you
Let them give you the honor and glory
Seminal
Searing
Seeking to praise you
With all one focus
All one heart
As we worship you
Giving you all the praise
All over the world
Bless your worshipers
Let the fire fall on them

Let them call on your name
Crying out to you
Wanting others to come
Worshiping
Angelic intonations
Breathing the angel' song

She wakes up in the morning and the first thing she says is I love you Lord
Hmmm God is good.

LET THE FIRE FALL OCTOBER 13, 2011

Let people praise you like a wall of fire
Don't let them stop
Let it continue
Constantly
As it comes up before your throne room
Let us shout for praise
Giving you the honor and glory
Worshiping
Till our hearts
Can no longer
Give us enough oxygen . . . And
We rest praising you
Our lungs are out of capacity
We are spent
As we worship thee
David danced before the Lord
Worshiping
Let us dance in our spirits
Fly in our hearts
Zoom in His love
Until we congregate together
Discussing our love for Him
His daily lending breath to our lives
As we sing louder
Unable to contain ourselves anymore

Reacting to His love

GOD IS SO GOOD TO ME OCTOBER 13, 2011

Let your glory come
Like a tree that falls to the earth
Bending itself
Saying Lord Jesus
I give you all the glory
You are worthy
I bow down before you
I can't live another day without you
I must praise you
And lean a hand to glorify you
As I feel the branches beneath my feet
And the cold earth spreading itself before the
The whole forest floor in reverential idleness
Waiting
For your hand to move
Oh see me Lord
Your hearth is on fire
Throw me in
Until I flame up
Burning Brightly
Cook something on me
Warm something good
Until the coals, embers appear
And I'm all used up for you
Nothing left of me
The Holiness of God then
Angels will call
Good morning how are you doing?
Then they'll say
We were waiting for you
We must go now
Come along
Your reward
Is waiting
Jesus is there (The joy of our salvation)
God the Father desires
To see you

Come (He is waiting)
Halleluyah, praise His Holy Name

Hark The Herald Angels Sing, Glory to The Newborn King

SONG TO PRAISE HIS NAME OCTOBER 13, 2011

1. Lah Lah LaLa LaLaLaLaLa Lah Lah LaLa LaLaLaLaLahh (long extension-up higher)	Be Still and know I Am God Be Still and Know I Am God
Lah Lah LaLa LaLaHada	VERSE 1 When you hear you'll know . . . . I'm near
Lah Lah LaLa La . . . hah dahhhh	Be Still and know I Am God
2. Lah Lah LaLa LaLaLaLaLa Lah Lah LaLa LaLaLaLaLahh (long extension-up higher)	Be Still and know I Am God Be Still and Know I Am God
Lah Lah LaLa LaLaHada	VERSE 2 As you listen to me, You'll find peace
Lah Lah LaLa La . . . hah dahhhh	Be Still and know I Am God
3. 2. Lah Lah LaLa LaLaLaLaLa Lah Lah LaLa LaLaLaLaLahh (long extension-up higher)	Be Still and know I Am God Be Still and Know I Am God
Lah Lah LaLa LaLaHada	VERSE 3 As I come in your heart, you will believe.
Lah Lah LaLa La . . . hah dahhhh	Be Still and know I Am God
4. 3. 2. Lah Lah LaLa LaLaLaLaLa Lah Lah LaLa LaLaLaLaLahh (long extension-up higher)	Be Still and know I Am God Be Still and Know I Am God

Lah Lah LaLa   LaLaHada . . . .   VERSE 4 Halleluyah, you'll know,
                                                              I am here . . . .

Lah Lah LaLa   La . . . hah dahhhh   Be Still and know I Am God

GLORY TO GOD OCTOBER 13, 2011

La La La   La La Lah   Lahhh
La La La   La La Lah   Lahhh

Worship Oh Mighty King
Everywhere the Creator sings

Da Da Da(up) Da Dah Da Dah
Glory to your Holy name

Da Da
Oh Lord

For all eternity sing to God
Our King

The God of Israel
Praise Him

You are Holy
My King

Exalted on high La La La Lahhhh . . .

Jesus   Da ah Da
The mighty One of Israel   La LaLa La La La LaLa
Reaching out   Da Da Da Dahhh
To me   Dah Dahhhhh

WHEN YOU PLAY FOR ME OCTOBER 14, 2011

Window of my soul
Open up shine your light on me
Break though the walls
Let me see
Tambourines falling all around me
As I dance to thee
Snow falls, joys of a thousand years
Tickle my ankles, listening to the things I hear
Waiting for your love to fall on me
Listening to the music while you play
Earnestly seeking my heart way
To come before you and sing
Halleluyah

GOT TO GET YOU BACK IN MY LIFE OCTOBER 14, 2011

Darkness arise
Come out of my eyes
I'm not the same person anymore
I've been changed by the cross
The blood shed for me
Now I fall upon the knee
Worshiping
Need you
Won't let you go
Living
For you
Blood shed
Red marker in the snow
Telling me
I need to get back
To where I should be
Notations
That fall on unwritten letters
Of my love for you

THANK YOU FOR TODAY OCTOBER 17, 2011

Ministering Holy Spirit has come down
Glorify thy name
Glorify thy name
Worship your name
Oh most High, Powerful
Almighty God
I breathe you
I come to you in the garden
Your fragrance puts tears in my eyes
I drink from your rivers
I rely on your banks to reassure me
That I can be safe when I sleep
Let me flow under the leaves of your tree
Waiting upon thee
In sweet supplication
Worthy is your name
Holy is the reminder of your grace

HE SAW ME OCTOBER 17, 2011

I'm looking out the window
Foreign columns beside me
Headed in another direction
Waiting for me to come out
Rain is falling
They hear . . . watching
Roman soldiers in the distance
Waiting
I knew Jesus had died
And they blamed me
For giving Him up to the Pharisees
I didn't get a chance to say goodbye
I took His love for granted
No more can I see His face
Condemned man they spoke in His face
I couldn't be there
I had to find my place

Where I had been before we met
Tangled, muddled, with a strange mindset
To get away
Torture
What have I done
I put an innocent life to death
He was my Savior and Lord.
Uncanny behavior
For one such as I
Before
And now I die
His eyes
Judas, betrayest thou the Son of man
With a kiss
My failure
When he loved me
He loved me
He . . . . loved . . . me . . . .

SHE CAN'T ESCAPE WHEN I'M LOOKING FOR HER
OCTOBER 18, 2011

The darkness is going to leave her life
And the light is coming back in
I saw her sleeping
I knew her state
Wonderment in sin
Under the grace of God
I told her not to do it
She went ahead anyway
Suffering
But I said child you are mine
Come back home to me
There is no-one or anything that
Can separate you from my love
I love you my child
Satan's devises and schemes
Are meant to harm you
However I have come to set you free

Touch my hand
Say "Jesus hug me?"
And I'll bring you back home, daughter
Back to my place of rest
Where you once belonged
And now will still be
Come back home
I'll give you everything
All the diamonds and jewels of this world
Will fade
The Light of eternity will shine
Then you'll see my glory

May we worship you the more Father and give you the honor and glory you deserve

ANGELS WE NEED YOU TO TELL THE LORD OUR STORY OCTOBER 18, 2011

Flying out
Looking at the clouds below me
Thinking back to what I have to do
Registering for another promo code
Always trying to win
Noticing what my friends are doing
You look in my eyes for truth
Nothing escapes your grasp
I am laid bare
What do you see inside me?
What have I done that's wrong in your sight?
It's in my heart, deep enough no one will see
You however fashioned me for your presence
You know my down sitting and uprising
Consider the lilies of the Field.
How they grow
Softer and softer
Listening to the Master's call.
Straining to hear His voice
Listening to His breathing

That breeds life,
Only you God can bring me back from the edge
When the dark night calls
And the grimy clingy hands of death
Jesus pushed away
Leaving that place
Called Unmentionable-Hell
To take back His people
That He loved
Revealing to Israel
I AM the Way, the Truth and the Life

It's me
I'm the Lord
Surely in vain they worship foreign idols
I gave them life
Then they turn and ask why?
Not knowing I see their endeavors in evil
How they come up to me with hands impure
And look to my face with a need
I show them the cross
And they turn away
Then ask me why?
I look at them then
Waiting
Watching
Wanting you to know
It's in worshiping me
That your answers will come

I'm here Jesus

Answers to prayers will come
When you get on your knees

Carrying the word of God
Means determination

She has an anthem in her heart
She's different from you
She welcomes me in her heart when she sings
Like a spiritual high she loves me
She doesn't get on her knees in vain
Like you do
I hear her voice in heaven
Yours is a tinkling cymbal
She's ready to go when I call her
You wait around

Blessed be the name of the Lord.

WHERE ARE YOU WHEN I CALL? OCTOBER 20, 2011 (DAD'S BIRTHDAY)

Nothing wrong
Just my center
Willingness to move
When I say
But there is to much in the storm drain
Letting others come inside
The flood of my mercy is quietly waiting
You've got to get on your hands to repentance
I called you this morning
But you didn't hear
Listening to the words of your sleep
Meant more than watching
And being with the one you love
You forget that I made you
To praise and worship me
Not a figment of your imagination
That comes and goes
I need you awaken
To work with you early
To hear your voice in praise
And warfare can began
On a higher level
Going deeper within the fight

As for you
The tanks are coming
But you don't see the storm
Because your eyes are fogged with nursery rhymes of the past
Cutting through the darkness in Your heart takes time
Didn't you see what I did for you yesterday?
Why can't you understand?
What transpires in your heart to cause such sin?
You need only turn around and look at the day
Then you would see
Why I have called you to be
They pass by
They don't know Jesus
Someone has to tell them
Where are you . . .
When I call?

Thank you God for revealing my heart to me

GOD GIVE HER YOUR GRACE OCTOBER 22, 2011

Cover her
In your praises
Let her love you more
Tears fall from her eyes when
She hears your voice
She listens
Take her to your secret place
Never let go of her hand
Listen to her
Leave her holding your garment

You took her aside to show her somethings
She made you happy
Bring her back even more happy
Her eyes are wide with your love
She's a different person since you saved her
When you hugged her with your love
And she shows it forth

It goes around the world
As she talks about you

Her voice makes your Holiness real
When she encountered you
Her heart sings your praises
Her mouth continually tells of your glory
Who can find a virtuous woman
For her price is above rubies

Bless this woman Father, never let her encounter shame or suffering and be a blessing to many

HIS NAME IS FOREVER GRACE OCTOBER 22, 2011

The power of God filters through the clouds
You feel the joy
But sing
You enlighten the soul
Like a recorder
I can never tell
What you will play next
It feels like the softness of the wind
When I look upon your face
Nothing can ever be the same
I am in the secret place
Before the holy throne
Getting what I deserve
Feeling like the river courses
Of your love
Increasing my being
Sustaining my inner man
Such love and mercy who can find
I can't stand the coverings and trappings
Of ungodliness
I rip away
My sin is before you
Cleanse me
Get me back down on my knees where I belong

I have become to mighty
To "big" for my own good
I must submit
Before the Throne of Grace
Where His blood flows out of His side
Reaching down to me
Piercing me
I can't let go of the cross

"Now you see, you're talking about me, now I can work in your life, before you came with all your worthiness that stinks in my presence, I wanted to see you humbled and now you are ready to see my plan."

Nothing but the Blood of Jesus, Oh precious is the flow that makes me white as snow . . . .

You are so Holy Father
Amen

<u>CAUGHT IN THE MIDST OF CHANGING CIRCUMSTANCES OCTOBER 24, 2011</u>

A miracle of God in the making
Somewhere lies beneath my innermost feelings
Dividing the wind and the sea
As the boat rocked back and forth
He called out to me
Come Peter

My hand drifted out first
Then my feet touched
What I couldn't see
And I walked-to Him
He smiled

The journey took a second
And then my eyes were fix on the waves
Fear set in

And then I fell
And cried out to Him
Lord saved me

His hands reached mine
And I felt I could live and breathe again
He pulled me out
Then the boat was at land
He told me not to fear

Thank you Lord you've told me and taken care of everything in my life

IT'S NOT ALWAYS WHAT YOU SEE OCTOBER 24, 2011

Caught in a storm
Looking down
Sea is wet
Waves abound
Frenetic and frustrated
We didn't know what to do
So we woke Him
From His sleep

He looked at me
Then at the others
Saying what's wrong?
I didn't have to say it
As he spoke to the winds and the waves
And they calmed
Then he looked at me
With eyes That wondered
Why didn't you do the same

O ye of little faith
I didn't know what he meant
I thought we were doing our best
But His eyes said
No, what I taught you should have used

I then began to realize it was all by faith
Everything He said-believing
For without faith
It is impossible to please God
Then I knew what he meant
Use what He's given me

I needed that Lord

JESUS PUT A NEW SONG IN HER HEART
OCTOBER 28, 2011

So open so realization
It goes into my heart
As she says the words
So caring and loving about God
She just wants people to know Jesus
No hidden, motives, objectives, agendas
Just right out front, Jesus is real
She cried as she explained Jesus
Could hardly put it into words
Talking about her lord and Savior
With all she knew
I wonder if clarity like that
Can make the whole world seek Him
Her voice rises on Holy ground
And the anointing falls
Then I need to be on my knees
Thanking you for life this day
And a heart after you
Open doors to bless her
May her eyes see your glory every day
And her heart give the angels a new song
To sing about their Lord
His blessings upon her

THE ENEMY'S GRASP BROKEN OCTOBER 28, 2011

Your Glory Lord
He is coming back again
Praise to the father
Worship Him
Among the heavens
Let his glory come
Let the angels bow
And the doors open
To praise the Lord
Hallelujah
Hallelujah
Music from Heaven
Sing praise, Honor and glory to the Lord
Worship his name
Praise
Praise
Glory
Glory
Angels
Worship
Worship
AAAAAAAhhhhhh,
AAAAAAAhhhhhh
IAAAAAAhhhhhhh
IAAAAAAhhhhhhh

YOU SHOWER US WITH YOUR LOVE DAILY FATHER OCTOBER 28, 2011

Cars flowin down the street
People we meet
Reachin out to think
About
The Lord in his goodness
Worthy is his name
We call out to thee
Saying Jesus fill our hearts

Touch us again
Make us kind to one another
When we see one in tears
Bring us back to the place where we remember
How good it was to hear your voice
When you lifted us out of the dung heap
Where we were situated
And could not dispel the gloom
We were captured by
Then the morning sun shone brightly
And my chains fell off
And I could see
He filled my life with
A joyous peace

Cameras flashing in the crowd
People calling out aloud
Jesus
Jesus
This is where I want to be
In the center of praise
And worship to you
Worshiping there
Dancing for you
Began the symphony of the Lord
Let Him sing into our hearts
I hear your voice calling
In the sanctuary
JESUS!!!!!!!
Angels are singing . . . . Yeah!

Music is in my ears singing Jesus

WHEN I LOOK AT HER I SEE JESUS ALL THROUGH HER OCTOBER 29, 2011

Jesus bless her
Just bless her God
I'm glad she came to you

Broken like a picture of glass
Jesus put her together again
Her fate was sealed
When he touched her hand
Priorities straightened out
Her voice now measured with grace
Now looking at what really matters
A different day
Her rainy days are at an end

Ceilings fall down
Crumble when they are old
Music stops playing
When the fingers are numb and cold
She looks at the day different
No more sin
Just Jesus now
Never more seeking the desire to sin
Her face looks up to Him
He sits on the throne
Waiting for her
To be in His Presence

LOST IN LOVE WITH HIM OCTOBER 29, 2011

Your glory falls down when we worship you
Crystalline portions fall down from heaven
When we worship you
Glass pieces that fragment our hearts
Shards that bring a reality of His grace to us
They make us realize the truthfulness of
His mercy and grace
Looking glasses to see
What we should be
We pick up a piece of glass vaguely
Looking at ourselves
We see a reflection of ourselves
In heavenly graces
Around the throne

About the four Living Creatures
Worshiping, saying
Holy, Holy, Holy
That's where I want to be
Worshiping
Amen

IN TIMES OF PRAISE MY SOUL WORSHIPS HIM
OCTOBER 29, 2011

Your Glory
Your glory God
Majesty on high
Hallelujah
Mighty one
Father of All
God of mercy
Ancient of Days
Filler of our hearts
One who holds the candlesticks in His hands
El Ralpha
Jehovah Jireh
Bright and Morning Star
Healer and Redeemer
Anointed one
Righteous branch
The Cornerstone
Laying at His feet
All your treasures and dreams
He is Holy
Worlds bow to Him
In adoration
He is Lord
Amen

Hallelujah for what you just did Jesus
Hallelujah Amen

<u>I LOVE THE LORD FOR ALL HIS GOODNESS</u>
<u>OCTOBER 29, 2011</u>

Bless you name oh God
Bless your name oh Lord
Bless your name Oh God
Bless your name oh lord
He is Holy
He is glorious
I have to praise Him
When I'm low
Nothing works
When he brings me out
I have to say
I need to shout

<u>HIS LOVE OVERCOMES OCTOBER 29, 2011</u>

Wash us over clean with your loving kindness
Let your Son shine on us
Despite the rain
We need your glory to come in
To shine on our faces
On our hearts
To make us new creatures
To wash us anew
Cleansing
Our souls to make real
Our love
In the rain
We want to have a revival
Nothing new
Just you
No more masquerading
Emptiness
Then allergic reactions to sin
Changing
Our being

Daddy's here
Hallelujah (Trying to get away, come here-tickle tickle, hee hee-Daddy)

WAITING UP, JUST WANTED TO HEAR YOUR WORDS OCTOBER 30, 2011

Sounds like it's time for Jesus
To look inside myself
Pull out what doesn't fit anymore
While I'm listening to a musician
I'm listening to Jesus speak
Different voice
Kindness-words of peace
Just thinking about you

Interpretation of mime signs
Aren't always written on paper
Maybe we aren't suppose to understand everything at once
Maybe it's His way of saying
I'm taking care of business, you sit still
Wait
When it's ready I'll tell you
Like cookies out of an oven

It makes me think of you
Watching Television
There is something on
And you're calling me to bed
Just when it gets good
But you're waiting
Maybe just to say Hi
He needs me to talk to Him

He is God after all, we owe Him that, He created everything

SHE'S THE ONE I SENT YOU OCTOBER 30, 2011

She's a consecrated holy temple
On that day
She'll be in white
Broadcasting to all she loves you
You will be in brown

Her hair will be pulled back
Her teeth white as snow
She'll be happy
News will spread around the world
Then I'll listen to your prayers about her
She will conceive your child
You will be happy then
Listening to my voice
She will make you very happy
I know a secret
Where you will be in a year
She'll be carrying your baby in her arms
Waking you at night to feed
Saying I'm to tired
And you'll get up in the night
And hold the baby in your hands
Praying for me to make them wise
I'll look at you then
And wait for you to pray to me then
Thanking me for another lovely day
Holy Is The LORD

Her temples will be laden with gold from afar
Her heart saffron
Her legs strong pillars that will enfold you
Her mouth seeking you entwining
Then you will give her a child
Myrrh is the beginning of your love
Trees of Oprah standing in your fields
You will do the duty of man
And He will impart to you life
Enjoyment will come
She will wait
Her eyes set upon your face
Desiring you

<u>WHY ARE YOU SO GOOD TO ME NOVEMBER 2, 2011</u>

He carried the cross
Of wood of gold
He carried it up
Calvary I'm told
He made it to the to
Of the tree
And stood there on it
For all to see
He bled and died for you and me
I couldn't go on with one day
Without thanking Him for
The price he paid
I sit here now wondering how
He didn't flinch
He didn't move His mouth
When I fall I look to Him now
Worship Him and ask Him how?
He gave of Himself thinking of me
When I did something and didn't feel worthy
He said to me
There is not a stain of sin I can't lift
If you'll remember
That precious gift-the Blood
Of Love-Shed abroad to all mankind
Peace on Earth find your joy in me this time

Thank you Lord, you make me cry sometimes

<u>WHEN SHE MAKES A MISTAKE I HEAR HER VOICE NOVEMBER 2, 2011</u>

SHE CAME TO THE LORD LAST NIGHT 8 PM GIVING HER LIFE
TO CHRIST NOV. 1, 2011

She sinned
She saw her failure
God knows her name

Her family line had
Darkness at the core
But Jesus forgave
When she said those words
Whispered thin-among the crowd
"Please Jesus I need you here and now"
I don't know what you want of me
Something's wrong inside of me
Longing for a change in my life
Wishing, hoping it's true
What they said about you

Break these chains forever
I'm through with sin
Lord I need your help
There's a baby inside
Don't take Him away
Don't let Him die . . . Please Jesus?
Please God
Remember the words I have said
I'll follow you everywhere
Til the end of earth
Don't forget your promise
You'll be with me
I need you now . . . please forgive me
Thank you Lord

"I forgive you my child
The baby Will Be
A kindly child
She'll wash in the morning
Listening to Him laugh
As she saids," "Thank you Lord"

Thank you Lord for her child
Thank you Lord you are so great
So kind, so generous, so loving
That you'll give her little boy life

To live on this earth
Oh Father you are so good
I praise thee
"Now go and worship me!"

<u>YOU'LL GET A REWARD IF YOU PERSERVERE</u>
<u>NOVEMBER 3, 2011</u>

You are my King
Wondering where I will be
Looking at the clock
Worried about tomorrow
All the things I have to do
When I could spend time with you
No other reason
Than putting myself down
Letting your words rebuild me
Making me a man inside
Taking me out of the course way of sin
Watching me kneel
I look at your face
When I'm down
Thinking maybe
I'll leave this life
The angels come near
And tell me then
When you look at me
You find the best
You made me what I am for a purpose
Never forget son
I'm in charge
Made you in the womb
Purchased you with my blood
Now why do you suppose
I let you live so long
I need you
To follow in my shoes
To be my disciple
Now remember

Agony, pain and sorrow I felt
To tell them I loved them
You have to experience the same
So I can show them
They can go through it all
And be purified
With you as the example
Don't be weary in well doing
For in due time you'll reap a harvest

Thank you Father, for you have been giving me a harvest
Thank you

You're welcome, now read my word.

I NEEDED YOU WHEN I WOKE UP THIS MORNING NOVEMBER 10, 2011

Moving mighty realms of paper
Caesar's signature
They said nail Him to the cross
His eyes saw them
They made no excuses
Just wanted Him dead
He was alone then
All had left Him
But His father
Nothing left that I could do
But give myself

It all started long ago
When he was a child
A crucifix in His future
To love so many
Then have them turn away
He looked at their faces
They wanted nothing more to do with Him
His blood flowed
They would have life if they only knew

The nails hurt
The pain
The suffering
The agony
And I wonder why do I look at Him
When he needs me to fall on my knees
And pray

The walls of the Roman empire crumble
His name is still held high
His glory is evident throughout creation
Angels sing His praise
People bow down to Him every Sunday morning
Many and women praise His name
And I live because he died
The stone on the tomb has fallen
he is no more there
You can't touch Him now
Only when you call
In pain and forgiveness
Bearing what He felt
Tears excreting pushed out of eyes
That didn't want to see Him until now
Oh Lord God, have mercy on me a sinner
I need your grace, I need your washing
I need your clothes, to be clean
Wash me in hyssop that I might be whiter than snow
The crimson flow from your veins
Repair me
I am undone
Swept away in the wind
With no course to follow
Bereaved of life
Living without an end

Burn within me deep inside
Renew me
My veins barely pump
my heart grows faint and weak

As I struggle the last steps
To get to your love
Naked I come
Heart franchises empty cases
Reeling from recklessness
Situated in a hard places
Stones around me
Walls I can't penetrate
Bust through to me
Breathing through a straw
Barely able
I need you
Completely

HE'S CALLING YOU NOVEMBER 10, 2011

You don't want a new thing to pass you by
You want to get on your knees and pray
And tell the Lord thank you
He sees it all
Nothing stands in His face
He is the Lord
There is none like you

HE WAKES ME FOR A CALL NOVEMBER 10, 2011

You woke me up this morning
Started me on my way
When I was stone-cold asleep
You set my feet on solid ground
On the narrow way
Only don't turn away
He keeps saying to me
One look, one glance
Is all it will take
To make you go back
Stay with me my child
And I'll send you to distant shores
Modeling-My will for you

THE BLOOD OF JESUS COVERS ME
NOVEMBER 10, 2011

I feel hurt
I feel pain
There is no answer
To what's going on inside me
It's like a river
Seeking to find it's course
Like a skyward startling
Worried about warming itself in the sun
How do I get to it?
Which way do I fly
Where is the sun when I need it?

He's here my child
Just waiting for you to worship me
Just waiting

JESUS, WHAT A WONDER YOU ARE
NOVEMBER 11, 2011

People's hearts come up to the Lord
While you sing to me
I hear them crying out to the Lord
Jesus I need you
You came to me
I want to open the door
Jesus look at me
See my face
Look at my eyes and my hands
Need me to be more like you

I hear their voices in the night as they sing to you Jesus
A song of joy
Singing I love you Lord
I need to be near you
Near your presence
Where I feel strong

Your love fills my heart
And the angels sing
And I'm in heaven
Gladly sharing what you've given me
Worshiping you worshiping thee

Loving you Jesus is what I 'm created to do, you are the effervescent flow of love washing my feet making me whole again. Oh Jesus, oh Jesus, ohhhh Jesus. Be magnified oh Lord. Be mag-ni-fied.

Angels are here in the midst, hallelujah, **He is the King**
Bring presents to Him
Adore His majesty
Bow before Him in this place
He is Holy,
Holy
Take your shoes off
Bow down before Him

In Praise
In Worship
More of me Lord
More of me
Angels are singing
There is a name I love to hear . . .
The sweetest name on earth . . . .
Oh how I love Jesus

Their singing this to you
For a reason
Ho—is calling
You need to get a phone
Hark the Herald Angels sing
You'll see why . . . soon
A—is calling
Angels are near
Now go . . . !

Yes Father God, yes Holy One of Israel
Thank you Jesus for your mercy and love

CLARICE' DREAM NOVEMBER 16, 2011

Little boys running
Throughout the house
Little girls sitting
Like gentle little mice
I see her sitting there
Reading the paper
Dignified in a way
Watching
Coughing
She knows who needs medicine

She needs a warm blanket now
She's cold
Tells me when her
Fingers hurt
Listens for our laughter and
Unspoken hurt
Prays that we'll be alright

A woman
That dreams
Of a man she loved
Of someone who
Has a present for her
Of Jesus
She wants-for His coming . . .
He's coming soon.

Thank you Lord for mom, bless her God.
Every footstep
Her later years
When no one sees her
Silent tears.

WHEN I COUNT IT ALL JOY NOVEMBER 16, 2011

Several people outside the door
Hallow—masks
Thanksgiving turkeys galore
Christmas comes
Full of cheer
A happy hour Happy New Year
Then we rest after the seasons
Lending our ears to relieve the tension
Of countless arguments though those days
Of watching for Santa on his sleigh

The woods
Are filled
With leaves under my foot
Weariness I hate to look
When I've stared down at my books
Hoping to find a treasure and a reason
Something to keep me occupied this little season
Thoughts dash here and beyond
Twining glasses
Of treasured days-Christmas song
I listen and I am left
Climbing the attic, reaching for the steps
Where all the secret things are kept
For you

SEEKING YOU OUT NOVEMBER 17, 2011

Wash away my pain.
Diligently serve me
I will

IF YOU LOOK YOU WILL SEE ME
NOVEMBER 17, 2011

When you listen to her you will get an answer
Darkness walls fall down
When you listen you hear
My voice coming to you
It pierces through the storm
And arrest your heart
Until you feel like telling me all
Then I can hear your voice
As you tell me the truth
Then humbly bow
As I work in your heart
Then you will see me dearly
As I portion you grace
Planned from the beginning
When you were a babe
Still in the womb
Then I called you
To live
To give
Out my word
To the starving
Needing
Beaten, downtrodden
This is where I AM

ATTENTION GETTER NOVEMBER 17, 2011

She sings
When she sleeps
I am not left without
Someone
Who gives herself to me,
On a daily basis
Your life is like a trombone
Noisy
You need to read John
Thank you Father

TRUE REVELATION SONG NOVEMBER 16, 2011

Ceaseless praise comes up to me
And you lay on the bed asleep
That song meant to many
About my glory
You were in another land
Oh sleeper
When will you awake?
The hands on the clock
Are saying,
It's getting late

Got a pager
Got a beeper
Maybe it will
Tell you the time
All semantics
As you sit there
Listening so blind
That you couldn't see . . .

This is a war on . . . .
Be on the best side
Should you choose me

CRYING OUT TO GOD EARLY IN THE MORNING NOVEMBER 18, 2011

Hear our voices
Let us look up to you
Let the angels move about in Heaven
And give us a blessing
Let your eyes look down upon us
As we say yes to thee
That our will be your will
Be answer-from our hearts, we will sing to you
Be my Lord and Savior
Let go of my past sins

Under the blood of Jesus
Hear our voices
As we cry out to you
Oh God
In desperation we cry to you
Have mercy on us on our souls
Hear our voices oh God
Send us your kindnesses
In Christ name we pray
Amen

THERE IS A NAME I LONG TO HEAR . . .
NOVEMBER 18, 2011

The angels worship you Lord
All evil moves away
Your voice is heard throughout the creation
As men worship you
And give you honor and glory
They turn around
With swords lifted high
Coming to worship you
Man looks out of the windows
And his eyes behold the glory
And they cry holy, Holy, Holy, Jesus Lord
Oh we adore you
Worship and praise to you

They Glorify my name
So I bless them
She sings with the Harp home in her heart
So I give her grace
She is my daughter
She is a joy to me
I hear your voice
Father bless her
So I can now make her more
Joyous
There is an angel that hears your prayers

And walks before the courts of the Holy Lord
And I give Him grace
Because you listen to my voice
And she will find strength in a day of trouble
She is an answer to pray for many
And my Jobe

Thank you Father for creating Kari Jobe,
Thank you oh so kindly
Your mercy endures forever

My lovingkindness is better than life

PRAYER FOR A SAINT NOVEMBER 18, 2011

Bless Kari Jobe Father
Bless Kari Jobe
Give her grace in your sight
Allow her to know you more
Let your glory be revealed to her
Touch her life with your joy
Let your glory descend
Thank you Father-please bless her Lord
In Jesus Christ holy name, Amen.

ANGEL PRAYERS NOVEMBER 18, 2011

I'm talking about an angel of God
She curls up beside me
Wondering what she's going to be
Hair all translucent
Nose and mouth
Little arms
Legs that spread
Out to me
A little angel yet to be
Dreaming of her place
In heaven
Where she will stand?

Whose child she'll watch?
Knowledge to Understand

Me
Her Lord and Savior

They will all fall and bow
She will wait and see
Before bowing down to me
How do we call Him?
She will say
They say **JESUS** is
The name we say.
She'll fall down and
Bow on her little knees
And I'll touch her there
On her little sleeves
She'll watch my face as
I smile at her
Then she'll smile back
In joy and mirth
Saying, dear Jesus—"I love you"
Then I'll snuggle her up
In my arms so wide
And say "dear angel"
You are my pride!

(God you are so sweet)

JUST TO GOOD TO ME NOVEMBER 18, 2011

Lord Jesus you are just to awesome
More than I can explain or
Comprehend
Just to good to me
Worship your name
Glorify you always
I can't get close to you
You are to much for me

Thank you for all you've
Done for me everyday
I can't begin to count my blessings
So much more than I can tell
Continual grace
That's all you give me
Forever blessing me
You're coming soon

I WANT TO BE LIKE YOU NOVEMBER 18, 2011

Your name is Holy
Too much in my heart to say
The music makes my hands worshiping
My arms
My mind is steady on you
Saying Jesus, God . . . .
And I can't stop myself
The worship
The glory
Make me want you more
Till there is no more left of me
Take me to that higher place
Where no one can see me anymore
Just you
Just you . . . .

THEY CAN'T SEE YOU TE NEED TO FEEL YOUR GLORY NOVEMBER 18, 2011

Science wrapped
Around Concept
Who is it who made us?
Understand this concept
Kept them thinking, looking
From forever
Forever how to find
That which they know
He is holy

Holiness is the Lord
Holiness is the Lord
Holiness is the Lord
Amen.
Yes come quickly Lord Jesus.
Hallelujah to your name
Hallelujah

WHEN HE SINGS I HEAR HIS WORDS
NOVEMBER 22, 2011

Music makes me feel down today
Staring at the notes
They don't make sense to me
Then he came and showed me
Then turnt the page around
And wrote His name on the back of the page
And now I can feel the rhythm
Between my fingers
And my voice has a lithe
Praising Him

Thank you Father

HE TOOK ME OUT FROM DARKNESS

He told me to get up
There was a nefarious smell
And He took me away before
My body ended
And took me outside
He saw what was going on
And said wait my son
The morning air stopped all
The burning and gave me back the life
Soothing me, telling me
Praise me

Worship your name and thank you God

WHAT PUT ME HERE NOVEMBER 28, 2011

It didn't help that I went to bed early
Nothing did
I'm away in trouble
Your anchor you cast to me
Desperately I'm drowning
Of my own accord
Licentiousness
Thinking
Thank you for having a part in my life
Knowing my wrongs
And patiently helping me to understand
There is someone at the door
Waiting for me
They need help
Why don't you see?
Every time I give you . . . a burden
You don't see the benefits
Of where I'm taking you
Storms will last for a while
You have to go through them
Then I can let go
And let you go through them yourself
Miracles abound
Like socks in a drawer
You have to open the door
To find them
They are around
Just look
Remember . . . higher level!

COMING HOME TO THEE NOVEMBER 25, 2011

We Praise you
And lift you high this morning God
We sing of your glory
All heaven does   La La LaLaLa Lahh
We call on your name

And Worship Thee
You are Holy
You are Holy   La La La Laaaa . . . .
You are God   Da Da Dahhh
Merciful Kindness all around
The Throne
Holy are you   La Lah La dahhh . . .
We worship you   La La La Lah
Lord of all   La La La Lahhh . . .
Holy One   La La La Lah . . .
Jesus   La La Lahhhhadah (Angels dancing)
My Savior   La La Lahhhh
My Healer
My Redeemer
Holy are you   La La La Dahhhh
Your face
Is Mighty
Jesus you are Lord of all   La La La Da Ah Lahhhh
My Holy One   Da Dah Da Dah Dahh
My Savior
Master of Israel
Messiah on High   LaLaLa Lahhh
Jesus Dah ha Dah
Father
Holy One La La La Dah
Whom we seek
Worship upon the Throne
Alpha and Omega
Bright and Morning Star
Glorious to be praised
All Glory and honor to Him
"We bow down before you Father"
"We are nothing you are all"
Holy is your name-we are but dust
You are God
Lift High the Righteous Banner
Let all Heaven adore
And worship Him
Forevermore.

For . . . everrr . . . more . . . .
Kay Lay Che Ah May Do
Master of Israel
You are Lord of All
Thank you Jesus

(Angels dance Touch Robe swirl in and out-Like ladies dancing back and forth-in and out, happy
filled with joy)

LISTENING TO THE AFTER EFFECTS OF YOUR LOVE FOR ME NOVEMBER 29, 2011

It went like a Monday morning
The searing tearing words
That pricked my heart
And left me in staring
Out the window
When music reaches the heart
And tares out the enemy strings
And pierces the darkness
It's Him
Not their voices
What he has put in them,
They can't stand it
It has to come out
And I am the recipient of their
Overflowing verses of lord to Him
Volumes of praises
Rising up
I am no more
An assemble that rises
Criticizing my being
Permeating my core
Lessons learned
I return to thee

You are enough Lord

IMAGINING THE WORST WHEN HE GIVES THE BEST NOVEMBER 29, 2011

Pieces of wonderment left on the ground
Sentences broken
Worried about the sound
He says hidden treasures are left for thee
Sun's coming
Winter's gone
Listening to the music
Worried about the sound
Believe the promise
Know that it's true
Walk downtown
Imagining the angels around
Listening for the voices
Then His words in the clouds
Tell them of me

WHEN SHE SINGS I HEAR YOUR VOICE NOVEMBER 30, 2011

Healing manifestations come from heaven
Streaming over her body
the milk of His grace
Removing any departure from the spirit
The agony she felt
Is gone away
And His mercy endures forever

Bless Annie today Father
Let her hands rise to you
As her voice sings of your love
And gives grace to the hearers

Send your Spirit to touch her
And rest upon her
Bless her this day

Thank you Father for Annie

A LITTLE DAUGHTER NOVEMBER 30, 2011

Blessing will fall on her like a waterfall
And Jesus will mention her name
In heaven today
There is an angel around her
That listens when the Lord speaks to her
And she sings His words
Like a fountain
They become like the healing wings
As angels move about her
Then the Father speaks
And she leaves souls-touched
By His goodness
When Kari sings
God moves in the Heavens

Let her know the Lord Loves her

THE DEEPNESS OF YOUR LOVE FOR ME NOVEMBER 30, 2011

You put words in my mouth
And make me sing
When I listen to you
My tongue begins to sing
The words formulate in my soul
And rivers of worship boil deep inside
Then the Spirit touches me
And the release
Frees me
Then I want to praise you more
And I can't stop myself
Praise you Lord
I can't stop praising you Lord
The words are deep inside me
You speak them to me all
And I have to pronounce your praise
The stillness of song

Near to you
Near to the cross
I bow
Blood running down
Shedding
Cleansing
Making me new
Centuries old song revived
I love to tell the story
Singing without backup
Grateful for today
She's a window that others might see you
"Kelly is mine"
Thank you Father for her voice is yours

YOU ARE MY GOD NOVEMBER 30, 2011

Wood strewn about
Carpenter's nails
Sawdust on the floor
He use to work there
Somebody's calling His name
A child across the way
Saying Jesus, I need you to fix . . .
He looks down at the lad
Lays aside His tools
And walks with the young one

Then on His death cross
The young one looks up at Him
And says Jesus
I was one of them
That shouted in the crowd
Listening to what the others said
Now I am ashamed
Why didn't I listen to your kind words before
You spoke to me

Jesus will you come once again
My soul is wretched
My heart is broken
There is an ongoing war inside
Healing, deep rivers you sent last time
I need your love to flow over me again
This time forever

Jesus cleanse me

"Worship" the missing piece
You desire
More than desire
He demands "we worship Him"
Amen

I worship you
I worship you
Almighty God I worship you

YOU SPENT TIME WITH ME JESUS
NOVEMBER 30, 2011

Two malefactors on the cross
One seeking life
The other not conscious
Of who stood with Him all that time
We forget to often
That Jesus stood with us
During those hard times
And we neglected to see His worth
We were staunch advocates
Against Him
Reeling in our own concerns
Populated with our thoughts of the present
To blind to see who was near me
Tears washed the ground at His death
The broken bones made me believe
That He stood with me

When I needed a friend
Someone to be there for me
This is my song now
He came when I was lost
Unable to fit Him in my schedule
The Lord of Glory decided to spend time with me
Now I know
He . . . spent . . . time . . . with me

Thank you Jesus

He spent time with me la la a da
Worthy is He la ah la da
Lord of Lords, King of Kings
He spent time with me

And the angels sing
He spent time with me
He is worthy
In the morning I sing to thee
You spent time with me

Holy is He
You spent time with me
When the angels sing
Glory unto thee
I worship you more and more
Because you spent time . . . . with me

Tears flowing
You spent time with me
When everything fell in
The pit I dug was very big
Your grace atoned and lifted my head
When you shed your blood . . . . for me

(Have Brooke Fraser sing this one)

MIRACLES ABOUND DECEMBER 1, 2011

River of blood breaking through
All the walls
Jesus welds a torch
Watches what is happening and sees
Where the work needs to be done
Flooding with grace
Cleansing my soul
Working within
Making me new again

Armies of God
Work in the midst
As nations come before Him
When we pray
He hears our prayers
As we worship Him
Bowing before you Lord
Saying Thank you Lord

The ones He sends working hard
To make me more like you
My heart empty of words
Fill up the desolate places lord
I can't remember to tell you how
Much I love you
Worship you Jesus Christ

I fall on the floor
Saying please Jesus
Let me worship
Let me into your throne room
Please give me the grace again
Don't let me wait outside the door and watch
Give me entrance
I bow and worship you

Hands raise arms lifted high
Please God
Accept my praise

"Now sit back up and watch the fire burn"

YOU ARE MY ALL DECEMBER 1, 2011

Song
I believe in you
I believe in you
Though things get hard
I believe in you
La La La   Da Da
La La La   Da Da
DaDa Dah   DaDa
La La La   Da Dahhhhhh

3x
I appreciate this song Lord

AROUND THE THRONE SONG DECEMBER 1, 2011

(Trumpets-Horns-royal majesty)
Bah bah bahhh ah dah
Here He comes Lord of All
Bah pa ah ah Dah
We lay offerings at His feet
La la la ah dah
As we worship Him

They line up before Him
Kneeling at His feet
Waiting for Him to touch them
And lift them to worship Him

The trumpets blow at His Presence
Everything will bend

When everything says
He is Lord
His name is Jesus

MAKER OF HEAVEN AND EARTH DECEMBER 1, 2011

Song
dada dada dadada dada daah daah dada

dadada dah dada da da da dada

Lord is coming soon

I worship you Lord

YOUR HOLY SPIRIT IS SO BEAUTIFUL DECEMBER 2, 2011

Healing and virtuous nature is within her body
She praises me in in the morning
I see her face by the windowsill singing
When no one listens
Perfected her
Made her dance when she sings
Her dialogues speak of my glory
She lives to represent my honor
When she speaks I listen
When Darlene sings they are like the stars of heaven together
Bless them Father
Give Jill and answer to pray today

HOLY GHOST PUT US IN THE PLACE YOU WANT US TO BE DECEMBER 2, 2011

The Holy Spirit pours forth
Out of the cisterns of my soul
Willingness comes to mind
To serve you
All the day long

You speak
When I listen
And I am encouraged
You bring me to
Mountain tops
And I thank you

SHE SINGS WITH HER HEART TO JESUS
DECEMBER 2, 2011

Her heart is open
Her soul is pure
So I can listen
To the prayer
She speaks
You can't hear her
But I know what her heart cried out to me
And I will give her grace
When she sings to me

Holy is the Lord, thank you Lord Jesus Christ, my Savior and Redeemer, He is
Lord

SHE HAS A NAME DECEMBER 2, 2011

Like a ballerina in the stars is her name
I hear her voice
She speaks she dances
I watch her anew
When she whistles
I call the horses of Heaven
And she wonders
At their mane
Then she rides
In heavenly places
Worshiping me
I love to hear Kari
Like a fountain of joy
Created

To give glory and honor to her Father
Watching His goodness
And blessing me
So she will hear my voice forever

EVERY MORNING I SING TO THEE
DECEMBER 3, 2011

Her prayers rise up to you in the morning
I hear her voice singing to me
While you are still sleep
She awakens to worship me early
In the morning light
When dawn appears over the horizon
When men still think of dreams
Her words steep deep
Like teabags immersed
Over and over again
She can't stand to be alone praising God
Her calling is to give others the grace
That they might worship Him
They worship me
Then I give her grace
When she awakens another day
They hear my voice there
And I give them more gifts of the Holy Spirit
When you sing
They will hear
Worship me
Over and over
Let the Spirit rain down

Oh praise you God, Holy One of Israel, Recorder of all dreams, Who knows our thoughts from afar, and hear our voices crying out in the night. He knows what the light causes the east wind to do, and the dragon' scales. He is a wonderment and I worship you. So descriptive and beautiful in nature. Holiness unto you. Admirable, let songs come up to thee when I sing in the morning light. Hallowed be thy name. Merciful kindness that exudes out of a doorway from His heart. He is Holy, He is God there is no other besides Him. Alpha and Omega the

beginning and the end, that exudes righteousness and holy fear. He is God. He is Holy and the exalted one. Ancient of Days, Bright and Morning star who resides in the heavens. Worship you, bow down upon our faces prostrate, worship you, glory God. Glory in the highest with His angels and creatures that serve Him. All bow below he is the majesty-the King. Stand before Him, straighten, be ready for His judgment, believe His words. They come from the altar-Flashes peals of thunder, your people Lord. Angels minister to them and your word be released from Heaven. Then quietness in your place as the fire hits the earth. You are to be worshiped and given the honor and the glory-mighty one. Righteous One, Merciful One. Divider of the day and when the stars appear, you loosed the bands of Orion.
Amen. Thank you Father

IF IT WHERE ONLY ME DECEMBER 3, 2011

The temple doors open
They bow before the man
Who is on the cross
A mile away
He looks at them with weary eyes
The Sadducees and Pharisees
They don't know who they crucified
They thought it was a man of dust
But the Lord stands before them
Worshiped and praised
Out of their distant eyes
They see
The storm clouds rolling in
And graves that will open soon
As He Restores creation
And the angels sing
Holy is His name
The Glorious One
Jesus is His name
he is holy
And the whole world sings
Glorious One, holy one lalala lalala
Jesus we love youuuu dada da da dahhhhh
You are the mighty God dada da dada da

Who shed His blood laa tha dada
When others fail
You gave me life
You brought me to the cross
To kneel before you
To say Jesus
Take my place
I kneel humbly before you
Can't you see my agony
I need you to take my place
I can't stand my sin
That weighs me down
While others watch
Me, sink in the mire
Call out to me
Resurrect me
Tear away my grave clothes
Your blood the deadness flees
Lead me to the death of self
Tear away my longings for the world
Until I serve thee fully
Losing nothing but gaining all
Please put your healing virtue on my hurts and sorrows
Forgive my sins
Wash me thoroughly with hyssop
Underneath-the joy of my heart is fulfilled

They saw the cross
Then the man upon the instrument of death
Breathe His last
And the temple doors shook
With the wings of His army
And the darkness came
Then the graves that couldn't stop themselves

AND THE VEIL WAS TORN
Making a way for us all
To enter the Holy of Holies
His Holiness

Oh angels bow near
And take our tears to **JESUS**
When we think of his pain
And sorrow
Forgive us lord
We crawl to thee
With tears streaming down our faces
With a cry in our heart
Why did it have to be thee?
If it were only me
But we were not worthy

Ahhh Hiiiii Ah Hiiiiiiiii

ONLY HE WAS WORTHY

Only you Jesus, Father of Glory, we bow down and give you glory, there is
no other who gave us His Son Jesus, Yahshua the Messiah.

Holy of Holies, Doors open to thee
Holy of Holies, Doors open for thee
Holy of Holies, let my eyes see . . . thee

ANGELS WORSHIP HIM DECEMBER 3, 2011

Holy of Holies
Bending down
Enter the tomb
No one is found
Jesus is Risen
He is Lord

Mmmmm God is good, He brings joy to me in the morning

ANGELS SONG AROUND THE THRONE
DECEMBER 3, 2011 SONG HOLY IS HE

Shem ma lo tov et sha tay nu
Shem ma lo tov et sha tay nu

There is a name in heaven
I long to know
His name is Jesus
(Drums) La dada da thay da dada
La dada da thay da dada
Jesus
We sing Jesus (angel dancing with streamers, in and out 16 lines)
Worship His name la . . . la La la
Worship His name
Worship His holy name

Jesus dant dant da ah they nu

His name is Holy,
Righteous one (dant dant background, still singing and dancing dant dant thay
da thay nu

Worship His Holiness
Maker of all   la La la la ah dah

His name is Jesus
He is the Mightyyyyyy King   la La La lahhhh la ah la

Robed in a garb of majesty
Author of our liberty

His name is Jesus
Almighty One

Da da dadada da da dahhh

Jesus
Jesus
Jesus

("He is Holy" background refrain said 3x time in concession earlier in song-quick
rapid pace)

I LOOK FOR YOU JESUS DECEMBER 4, 2011

She was a child in the wind
Didn't really know what a child was
She heard the angel
And began a new life
Saying my son shall be called Jesus
And everyone will call me blessed
I am grateful to God for all He's done
I don't deserve such goodness from God
He is all who created me
I am His maid servant
Be it as you have said

Be it as you have said in my life Lord
The things you planned for me
When I thought I knew the way
It led me astray
But your will is divine
There is a secret place you want to take me
I can't get there by myself
Where you will talk with me
And show me
Where I need to be
Take me

WHEN THE WINTER COMES A BABY LAYS IN THE MANGER DECEMBER 4, 2011

In a manger
Baby born
Loosening the grips
Of what the devil's torn
To shreds
My soul
But God has placed me in His care
When on a manger the child they bare
Looked down at the shepherds
And said a sound
That made their hearts leap

Refrain
For he was a child in the manger
That changed that holy night
Gave Himself for me
Took away the pain and the strife
Teaching me to love
When he cried from above
Nailed to the wood of brown hue
Forgive them Father
They know not what they do la la lala la la nu

I went to the city of Bethlehem
To see where the child lay
Then looked in the city
Seeking the star for the way
It stopped over a town
Called Bethlehem
Where I found the child
In a stall on the ground
Then He said in a whisper
A gurgling noise
It is well, as he smiled
And the angels rejoiced

Thank you Father for your mercy

SHE SINGS AS GOD REASSURES HER AND TOUCHES HER HEART DEC. 4, 2011

As her hands are lifted to you
I will praise you
And worship you
As you touch that part of her heart
Where darkness resides
I will ever give you praise
For you see
There is an answer
And she will be blessed
I praise you for using her

And thank you for taking away the pain
Jesus you are Lord of all

There is an answer to prayer coming to her now

Christmas time is a manner of grace, not to be taken lightly. Enjoy.

You look at love as if it is a tangible thing, it's not like that it's ephemeral. You have to receive and accept it. Then let it become a part of you then exude His goodness and Holiness to others that need to feel His love. Thank you Jesus. Amen.

Toy shop in Heaven, that's where people really get their toys. They sing up there and the colors are really vivid, nobody has seen God's workshop stuff you have never seen beautiful Holiness reds, greens, striped, blue ceiling, streets of gold, It's beautiful there that's why the lights attract you so, you are seeing me an answer to prayer for many. I'm Jesus.

Jesus is love
Come hear
Show you
See this
What is it?
Angels watching
Your Sword
Use it
Thank you Father
Just read my word, I'll take care of the rest

Close the curtains
He has to go
Shhhh it's bright and happy up here, it's Christmas time
The angels are singing
La la La Ahhh lahhhhh

Thank you Jesus, Father, merciful one. You are kind and good. I can't get enough of you. Miracles abound when you tell them of me.

Bye

A KISS FROM GOD DECEMBER 6, 2011

A Kiss from God in Heaven is like the angel's gate
The stars shine brighter
The moon beams louder
And they fly in joy
Ceases them in His love
He holds them in his hands
They love coming before Him
Beneath his Throne room
Where Falls of grace are abundant
And His mercy never ends
To all who fall on their knees before Him
He is Lord
Oh God the beams shoot out from Heaven
Your smile is infinite grace
Oh worship you Mighty Father
Among the lively stones
Burning brightly
Seated Highly and adored
Upon His throne
As Heaven adores
Righteously Ruling
Bringing under subjection all who are prideful
And lifting up all who are downtrodden
Bringing joy to their faces
And lifting their smiles
For you know where their joy abides
And how to give a song to their lips

God of Abraham (Slowly soft music)   La La LaLaLahhh
We worship thee   La Lah ha dahhhhhh
Mighty God   Da Ha Dahh
We sing to thee   Da Da DaDahhh
Holy One   Da ah Da Da
You are worrr-rr-thy   Dah Dah ah Dahhhhh

Mighty God   Dah Da Dah
We sing to thee   Dah da dah deeeeeeeeeee

You are
Holy
Mighty God
Of Purity
He came down from
The cross above
Letting His love
Be shown to all   (Song to be sung by Francesa Battistelli)

Oh God I never knew you were like that, so good and your mercy endures forever. Why do I stand up sometimes, I need to kneel at your presence without saying? No more of me just my heart rise to thee, like a paper kite flying up in your love. Back and forth just floating up on realms of your joy that can't be hidden for all to see. I love thee. Why can't we put more words in our dictionary to worship you, there are so few? So few . . . If the world cannot contain thee, how much more . . . ? How many times will I worship thee before all the heavens and say a few words that bless thee?

Just worship
(That's what I like)

Mmph so good

If the world where a marsh-mellow I would eat you up

HE IS WONDERFUL DECEMBER 6, 2011

You are worthy of praise
Many will feel your glory
And bow on the floor
To King Jesus
He is so beautiful
So beautiful
The angels sing before thee
Holy, Crown of Glory
Majesty
Beautiful Gracious One
Honor, glory, power, wealth
And strength to thee
Our King

HE IS THE GOD WHO MADE ME SEE
DECEMBER 8, 2011

Temple doors open
A song is sung
When Jesus comes
And we fall upon our knees
Waiting for His presence
To illuminate our circumstances
When we can't see
Waiting for a hand to lead us
Money to be thrown in our jar
I hear a call
The sound of many rushing
I ask them
Jesus the messiah is coming
I open my hand
My staff pushes me up
Noise
Jesus, thou Son of David have mercy upon me
He stops
They carry me before Him
I seek to have sight
My eyes are open
The people watch in amazement
He has my heart
Now I see Him on a cross
I wish I had never been given the ability to see
As He hung their without shame for me
I live because he died
And I see Him in agony
"Let Him go!" I want to say
But it is His time
His mother cries
Tears well in my eyes
He was crucified
His grave is empty
The tomb now gone
Angels of mercy all around

I see them talking
Then women hear
Shouting the noise
He isn't here
Running to tell Peter
And the ones inside
The Lord is risen
I watched their faces as they invited me in
Thomas doubting and then
Beholding His hands as He appeared
Jesus spoke "Blessed are those who believe
The Son of Man lives
I went home that night
Really in fear
That Jesus was God
And He had given grace
I lay on the ground
When he passed
No idea who was coming to me
He was Jesus, I was not worthy
That He should have touched me
He Is Lord

FAITH THROUGH THE STORM-WHEN JESUS COMES

(MAKE MENTION OF THE PEARL HARBOR INCIDENT)
The ship was overturned
And lives were lost
And we were afraid
But he said
Fear not
And our nation prospered
And we became
He reminds us
That a sacrifice long ago
Gave us life
When we feared no one could help us
And give us a hand

When none bothered
And to say
We are in this together
You will never be without me
For I will never leave you nor forsake you my Son
My Daughter

Amen

WHEN I NEED TO BOW MY KNEE
DECEMBER 10, 2011

Tensions of grace
Walling down my face
Fears beset me
Scorners in the midst
They look at me waiting
For my foot to slip
Saying Jeremiah
Don't say those things to us
Leave us alone
Let us live in our lusts

But like the fire of god within me
I must speak
I must tell them of God's will
That He sees their sin
When they worship idols
Falsely prophesying again
They will not eat again of this lands
Taken away to a foreign place
Carrying their garments shame on their face

They have left the Living God
So there is no place to be
Taken away prisoners
To a place they don't want to be
I am left alone-
With few in the land

As I watch them be carried away
By soldiers without fear
Who has left us desolate
And the temple gone

I bow my knees in prayer
Asking the Lord
To give them mercy
Beseeching with my soul
For his remembrance of the covenant
And kindness to this Holy Place
With knees bowed and arms prostrate
Begging His will be done
His eyes see their misery
Heal them of their sins
Returning to the heart of God
Help them Lord
Help them . . .
Have mercy . . .
Have mercy . . .

Oh God of Israel

SOMETIMES I FALL DOWN BEFORE THEE
DECEMBER 17, 2011

The purpose of God's heart is a good one
He now knows the wonders of my joy

Flooding my soul with tears
The Maker of all
Swelling inside with newness of life
As I fear and fall beneath Him to worship
Saying Jesus
Heal the inner man
Wash me clean inside
Make my heart glow inside to you
Give me reverential grace

Let the sun and moon and stars
Give you glory
And the angels shall come and worship you
And you shall light up the heavens
As your glory streams
And I fall down
In adoration
My heart leaps at the sound of your joy
And letters turn on the page
As I read your word
Then prayers come with syllables
That start from your heart
Without ceasing
Flowing up to you
In a heavenward way
That consistently fills
With the heart causing
A flood of grace
Purchased by your wrist strought veins
That where pierced by nails
Hammered
To the back of the cross
As you lay bleeding and dieing
That we might live
For an entrance in

Oh Jesus why did you do it for me?
What caused you to care for me?
When you where put upon the tree?
Why did you take my place
When you could have been set free
And given pardon?
Yet you took the life given to thee
That I might survive
Giving mercy to all
That worship thee

Oh Jesus why for me?

Because you are my son
Inheritors of my grace
That others might see . . .
"Me"

I SING A SONG OF GLORY TO THEE
DECEMBER 17, 2011

Just worship your name God
When I sit alone
I listen to you
Waiting for my heart to bleed
When I hear your voice calling
When no one else touches me
Then you are alone with me
And I'm happier than I've ever been
No one knows what we do
When we're together
When you touch me in the morning dawn
When I touch the floor
And you say "worthy"
It is like a lamp to my feet
And I cleanse and wash
Then wait on thee
Rivulets of your love flow down to me
In the cracks
I feel your mercy and grace enhancing me
Flowing with your love inside of me
I shout
Jesus, you are Lord of all

TEACH ME YOUR WAYS OH LORD (HIS GLORY)
DECEMBER 17, 2011

Oh Lord we kneel before
The angels they sing
Canon to thee
They sing

Glory
We wait
Petitions before your throne
People singing
Harps touched by the angels
The Holy Spirit resides
Angels awaiting
People on earth worshiping
All glory to thee
Angels walk
They talk
They hear
Praising
We cry out
And the heavens tremble
Somebody is making their way to the Throne Room
It is Jesus
Our God
He is crying out telling our needs
And making . . . . **intercession**

NO MATTER WHAT THE COST DECEMBER 17, 2011

Oh the covenant blood
That came streaming down
From his crown
To His chest
Heaving of "hurt" for me
Oh God I look away
You took so much
When I made so many mistakes
And gave you pain
I remember how I never said hello
Didn't even thank you when in the morning
When you allowed me to open the door
To see your glory
As your love flowed over me

You taught me grace
When I was alone
Saying this was what
You were given
When I returned to the throne
Now you worship me
As I stand waiting
For you
To give love when
You stand with your heart in pain
That they may see
I have given you grace

SOMETIMES YOU NEED TO BE REMINDED
DECEMBER 17, 2011

Oh Lord
You are so Holy
Only with your scepter can I arise
I cannot rise from the ground
You are worthy of all praise
I dare not look upon thee
For thou art King
I tremble at your presence
When thou pass
My eyes are closed
For you stand and all cry "Holy"
"HOLY IS THE LORD OUR GOD!"
"WHO IS, WHO WAS, WHO IS TO COME!"
"HE IS HOLY!"

How can you stand mortal . . . be of great fear!
For you are chosen
For His will
Fall prostrate before Him
BE READY
Hearken to the voice of the Lord
They don't see the times
It's getting darker by the hour

They need to know
Before, that judgment is coming
Be ready
To tell them
When they think not . . .
Sudden destruction

Cry out for the nations
And maybe I will relent
Of what I AM about to do
To the city and the people you know.

Most merciful Father, have mercy. Do not do that which you think to the nations. Help us to bow to thee.

I WILL HAVE MERCY THIS TIME

Oh thank you Sovereign Lord, Righteous-Most Holy God-you are worthy of praise, Hallelujah.
Kindness, Hallelujah, Jesus Is Lord Amen.

WHEN I SHALL BOW IN HUMBLE ADORATION
DECEMBER 17, 2011

Glory to His name
Thank you Lord Jesus Christ
Hallowed be thy name
Praise you in the courts of heaven
Make glad all who come to you
For you are the mighty one
Sovereign lord
Maker of all creation
Fairest Lord Jesus

Now I know you care about me
So the storms will pass
Then you will see
What I have in store for thee

Thank you Father
Thank you so very much
"When I consider all the work of your hands
Then sings my soul, My Savor God to thee
How great thou art" *

Thank you Jesus
Amen
Hallowed be thy name
HalleluYah

IN HIS KINGDOM DECEMBER 17, 2011

You threw the rocks at me
And it hurt
He lifted me
From the dirt
My eyes where closed as they condemned me
I opened them when
You set me free
Your love brought tears
Away from my eyes
My head was bowed as I looked at your feet
You spoke love down and lifted me to my feet
I washed my hair and put on new clothes
I started out again where no one knows
I was different then
I had sin no more
My hair was braided
As I sat on the floor
He said neither do I condemn thee
I went down to my knees
Worshiping Him please Jesus please
Be my Savior
I know you died on the cross
I remember your love
When all was lost
You took the nails
They put in your hand

Worshiping the Father
The Son of Man

I wiped my tears away
On your robe
Still crying deeply
A wound in my soul
Then you saw me
As I neared the tomb
Taking my hand gently
As you did before
Writing in the sand
Hatred you ignored
As I sat in the midst
The sun beating on me
You wrote a little list
And spoke about me
They listen then thought
I was surprised at their reaction
They dropped the rocks
And dispersed as a faction
Please Jesus Please
I said forgive me in my heart
He washed away my sin
And granted me a part
In His kingdom

I HAD TO LET GO WHEN HE TOUCHED ME
DECEMBER 17, 2011

My neck stretched up to look at thee
The one who spoke and set me free
My hands reached out
To the one who made me
You took me in
When I had no place to go
I was consumed by your love
When I took your hand
Crying for mercy

As you grasp and helped me from my knee
The look of love in your eyes contained me
There were no accusers
They had all gone and fled
The notes in His voice
Touching my conscience red
This life I put away
It had to end
When he touched my face
And said never again
Never again
Never again

UP ON THE CROSS I SAW WHAT WAS MISSING IN ME DECEMBER 17, 2011

The blood dripped down
When I was lost
From His head to His foot
Not one drop was lost
It all pooled before Him
As they looked on
Jeering
Saying
Come down Son of man
His arms extended
Stretched to their limits
As dice was played by
The soldiers uninhibited
Of the lowly scene
Of Christ life riveted
By the men around Him
Hanging nearby livid
Saying if you are the Christ
Take our pain away
They missed the point
Until one said
With a change of heart
He is just and wanted to be remembered

By Jesus-when he was dead
It took a toll on the
Son of Man
But even then
He did not relent
But said to Him
Today you will be with me in paradise

I scratch my head when I consider the matter
How did He love, when He was in tatters
It didn't matter
What was said
He responded in love
The long hours he bled
Blowing away what I consider myself to be
Acknowledging He must go deeper in me
So much deeper in me
So much
More what I want Him to truly see
I need Him to become . . . . me

YOU ARE GLORIOUS ONE DECEMBER 17, 2011

Jesus you came out of the grave
And I was alive
I couldn't fathom
All you did
As angels came down
And spoke about your rising
First to Mary and all hiding
Afraid together of what had passed
Then they saw Him
And knew it was true
HE was ALIVE
And teaching them still
About why He came
They set dismayed
As one faltered
Saying he wouldn't believe

Until he touched the Master
Jesus appeared after then
And told him "touch me"
My hands and my side
That he might believe
And His love go forth
To many nations
To many nations

Oh Jesus I love you, Jesus I love you, you paid it all upon the cross. Wonderful Lord, Almighty God-Father. God you are so good, so good to me. You came when I needed you. You were well aware of my situation and made the answer to the storm before you sent me in it. Hallowed be thy name forever.

CLEANSING MY SOUL DECEMBER 18, 2011

Worship all day cleanses the heart
Anger, issues, darkness
The light pierces
And rises from being flat in the boat
Somber thoughts of the past
Where there should be fullness of joy
Then He can give
Grace

LEAVING IT ALL BEHIND DECEMBER 18, 2011

They don't see what I am undergoing
Something within crying more
More of you Jesus
I can pay the cost
Worshiping you
What a minor cost
There's a name I need to know
. . . Yours

A CLEAN HEART DECEMBER 23, 2011

There is an error in your ways
That is not good to me
It's more like a mindset
Desiring
When you should be worshiping me
Don't you know
I listen to your prayers
I hear elements of

Get your head together
Deep six all the other thoughts and memories
You're listening
But working your heart preparing the ground
For pure worship

I SAW YOU SLEEPING DECEMBER 23, 2011

Saturn turns with rings
A lesson in the night
When we are looking
There are answers to be found
Not a Lord of yesterday but today
Answers are coming
When the dawn rises
And worship
Falls
From a grateful heart
Jesus there is no place I would rather be
Than with you

WORSHIP ME DECEMBER 23, 2011

Laughter of children
Stalking me
Desires of the flesh
I didn't see
In Pilates vision

Hands were washed
To get rid of me
Blood and heart
Reigning down
From the cross
A joyous sound
It is finished
Before you touched the ground
Your body three days entombed
Door shut stone around
Then the angel came
To open the tomb door
And you looked
Glorious
When we saw you again
I cried
When you touched me
Then sat down
And heard you talk to me
Saying Peter . . . .
I am restored
Why did I run away?
A lyre in my soul
Plays a song to thee
Of whispered thanks
Of worship to thee
"Now go!"

Thank you Lord
You are so beautiful

"I know"

To good to me sometimes, to good.

I PUT YOU HERE FOR A REASON
DECEMBER 23, 2011

My angel is working overtime getting you straight
In the morning light
Tearing up the ground
To give you
My grace
That you might be used
Fervently
Helping others
When I see
Their heart broken
When tears well up
And drop from their faces
And they cry
Then you come to me
Saying
What wilt thou have me to do?
And mercy reigns down
From my heavenly shores
Letting love furnish them with grace
That's why I have called you to me
"Now go!"

YOU ARE HOLY DECEMBER 24, 2011

Angels bow beneath His wings
I listen to their song
As they carry me
To your door
I listen
Then call your name
Angels around you
Dancing in your heart
As we sing to you
Creating a change within
That I might see you clearer
Then feel the darkness depart

While you bring me to everlasting
Places of your Glory
We worship you there
Calling your name
Jesus
Jesus
Jesus

SISTER OF GRACE DECEMBER 24, 2011

Internal cares in her heart are weighing her down
She's reminiscing about things of the past
Wondering what she might have been if.
But I will take her away
From this thought train
To believe
She's not like all the others
Her anointing was given to her
When she was young
Then calling "Hi Jesus"
Such a child
When her voice
Listen
She heard me saying
I'll take you places
Don't let your guard down
When she calls I hear
I listen to her guitar playing
When her soul hurts saying
"Jesus"

You are blessed
You will see a daughter soon
Brooke

THERE IS A LORD WHO WAS CRUCIFIED
DECEMBER 24, 2011

(Irish jig tune)
A dittlely dance, A dittlely dance
You say, you say
Da Daht Dah da da Dant da da
Dah Dah dah Dah
The King is coming soon
You say You say
Ba bop bah ba dah dittlely dah
You say you say

He's coming soon da dah dot da
Before you know Dot-dah do-doe
Dah dot dat dah da dittlely dah
Da-dah tay dah-da
Are you ready Da-dot tay da-dah
Da Daht Dah da da Dot dah da dah
Dah Dah dah Dah

Holy Holy is His name
Dah da tay dah da
Worship Him on High today

Set them free
The ones in sin and agony
Ba bop ba dah da
Upon the cross His thirst received
The vinegar made for me

I humbly bow and worship thee
taking away the sting of death
When you bowed the knee
Rising up three days giving me . . .
Life

Jesus is Lord.

Highly praise Him
Forevermore
Harpers singing
You are Lord

Worship, Worship
Worship you Lord
Ancient of days
We adore

GOD . . . THANK YOU DECEMBER 24, 2011

There is a God
Who sits in Heaven
While we sleep
Waking us in the morn
Walking us down the steps
When our feet are bare
Sending His angels to care
As we dance before Him

We dance
We dance
He's towering over our problems
Grabbing our hands
Like the Author of our faith
He sees all
Letting us know
There is danger ahead
And finding us a place
To lay our heads

I NEED YOUR HANDS TO MOVE FOR OTHERS TO HEAR DECEMBER 24, 2011

You are singing out loud
While angels dance up to me
Worshiping

Healing graces
Going out every where
Then you say "Yahweh"
His glory comes
Then He is pleased
The people magnify
His chariots come
And they sing with you
"Holiness unto the Lord"

Thank you Jesus Lord

JUST WORSHIP DECEMBER 24, 2011

YAHWEH
Mighty protector
Strong to save
Rescuer of widows
Deep is your darkness
Holy are your ways
Dear one of Heaven
ANCIENT OF DAYS

RETURN ING TO YOUR FIRST LOVE DECEMBER 24, 2011

SON of God is here
He is looking at thee
Worshiping me
Daughters of God
You pray for every day
But you forget the
One who gave His life for thee
Stand up
Praise and worship him
Then look into His eyes of grace

Angels worship me
I Am the holy One

The Master of Israel
Upon the Holy Mercy Seat
Why don't you call out to me?

Forgive me
Oh Holy One of Israel
Lamb of God
I worship thee
Forgive me
The nails on your feet
I bow before thee
In humble adoration
Have mercy on me
Please Lord

Diadem, crowns on your Head
Oh worship you Lord
Robe in scarlet red
Hands adorned in bracelets
Robed in white before thee
Singing Loud and saying to thee
Thou art worthy and Holy
This is what I want you to remember
This is what I want to hear
When you set your voice
In Adoration
As I set upon the throne
Worship Me

I know that my Redeemer lives
I have such joy today
La la la lala lah la lahhh
Lah la la la-la lah la

Thank you Lord
Amen

(Chloe Summers sing)

CELEBRATING IN HEAVEN DECEMBER 25, 2011

They are happy dancing and celebrating in Heaven
Presents He gives out in Heaven today
The angels are gladden
He holds the royal court open
The Earth receives His joy today

WHY CAN'T YOU SEE ME IN HER DECEMBER 29, 2011

When you where not understanding her
You thought you knew what you needed to do
When I was on the cross
It wasn't your hand that made the skies open
So who do you think you are?
What makes your shoulders higher?
What if I took everything away from you?
Why do you look down
On the people I sent you to?
Why don't you help them?
Ask me to have mercy upon them?
Instead of making yourself to be seen by men.
Why are you listening to songs
That speak of my goodness
But don't interpret my love
When someone needs you to take them by the hand
And show them me.

ONE WHO LOOKED, ONE WHO COULD NOT LOOK AWAY DECEMBER 29, 2011

A floor show
She danced before me
Dressed in white
I couldn't keep my eyes off her

She danced with a certain lithe
That made my eyes water
I could have her as queen
Go! Ask her what she wants
The head of the Baptist they say
The King listens
He's ashamed but for his oath's sake
He has the Baptist's head cut off
And given to her mother's clutches
Who desperately wanted him to stop
Telling the truth, about her.
But he listened
And heard the news
Then went away to a solitary place
To be alone
They came to see Him
This Shepherd
And He saw they were without a shepherd
Then began to teach
They listened and were attentive
When they tired
THE FATHER gave them to eat.

Thank you God for your words of Life

YOU ARE WAITING FOR ME DECEMBER 31, 2011

I'm trying to find you
Dust in the wind
Memories of you and me
When I look out the door
Castles fall
Then remembrances go
Shadows fall
White doors open
Then I sing to you
Where are you Yahweh?
Where is my laughter?

Watching you sing to me
That's why you can't hear me
Your song is lonely
I need your voice to be loud
Just different
Listen to my voice
Then work out your salvation

WHEN HE SPEAKS TO ME WHEN I'M READY MARCH 6, 2012

Armies will fall on a given day
The earth and heaven will sing this way
That the glory of the Lord has been shown around you
And you kneel before me
When you sing to be
Glory hallelujah
Precious King
Concerts in heaven
To the Dayspring
My love is for you
Forever and always
Now sings the Prince
The Ancient of Days

That's nice God, thank you Jesus
Must keep going
That's how Jill gets it, she rests from weary battles, then I give it to her
Believe, worship
Now let's go

WELL DONE MY GOOD AND FAITHFUL SERVANT MARCH 28, 2012 SONG

Well . . . Done

Well done
As He speaks into my ear
He tells me "I am near"
Well done

You call upon my name
Saying it's not the same
You've come through the rain
Well done

Well done
I am proud for all to see
What you've done for me
Well done

There He stood for me
In His Throne room I can see
All the angels gathered for me
Well done

Well done
My good and faithful servant
Who showed His love for me
Well done

SONGS OF THE HEART PART 2

Open the floodgates, compel them to come in, compel them Oh Lord to come in

IMMEASURABLE LOVE TO THEE OCTOBER 28, 2011

They can't hear me singing
Winter's coming
My soul is damaged
I've got blood everywhere
Angel of darkness around me
The enemy's throne mismatched
I need to be set free
Jesus help me
Out of my prison of sin
Catastrophic circumstances
That well up around me
Blinking back the tears Lord Jesus
Bowing on my knees
Take my place
On the wooden cross
Was my sins
Nailed to thee
Oh Jesus my lord
Purge me
With Hyssop
Never let me sing
Without joy
Immeasurable Love to Thee

<u>OH LORD YOU ARE THERE OCTOBER 29, 2011</u>

Blood runs cold
She's sees her disgrace
I knew a day
When she heard my voice
Now she longs
For the trappings
That killed her soul
Eva where are you now?
They all play your song
When you knew no wrong
You gave me your heart
Then said you aren't healing me fast enough
From the abuse
When they took me
Not letting me go
Raping my body
Taking me apart
Calling me names
I said Jesus where are you?
When you heard my voice
You brought me through
When I couldn't sing
Or look up to you
You told me
When time passes
I will see he gets justice
"The murderer . . ."
I hate him . . . you say
The judge should not have given him . . .
Any years
Death would have been nice
But I know
What he needs child
When he wanted a friend
Your father said no
He didn't need to know
This would have made him different

If someone had just said . . . "Hi."
He never let others know how he felt
Kept it bottled inside
Instead of reaching out for help
I know he's a murderer
They took your virginity
I need you to look at them in another way
When I went to the cross
They called me names
Said something amiss
Things words can't frame
And I took it upon myself
To call their names
to the Father
To have mercy on them
Even when they hated my guts
Searing pain as they made me walk Golgotha
Enduring the shame
The pain
To Love
All of you
My Lord, my God, why where you so merciful and loving to a wretch like me.
Because I AM
Lord forgive me, have mercy on those who persecute me, I am so ashamed
Why do you think I came for you?
You are so merciful
When you love someone, they may go through things but you are there,
You are there

TRYING NOT TO BE DECEIVED NOVEMBER 6, 2011

I feel in my heart something is wrong
but I can't put my finger on it
Something in the way
Something that's just not there
Usually I hear Him
But today it's cloudy
Different, soft

Where do I go from here
Why do I listen to all the words
When I can't hear where they are coming from
Only God knows
And I trust He'll tell me

JESUS TAKE MY HAND NOVEMBER 8, 2011

Listening to the morning
Waking up
Wanting to know you
To know more
I awaken my heart is moving about
I move to praise you
Then I began to see
You want me to go further
And I get into your courts
waiting
I need more
The day won't last
If I don't get enough of you
Like a starving man
Like a prospector out to find gold
Got to get enough
Everyday

Don't stop when the waters rise, overflow, we need an overflow

AROUND THE THRONE SEPTEMBER 19, 2012

Radiance is coming down from heaven
Their faces sing to the Lord
As they move about
Cherubim with their wings
Singing Holy, Holy, Holy
Before the majestic thronef
Singing eternal Hallelujahs
Around the sacred throne

Thank you Jesus.

<u>INNUMERABLE BLESSING UPON ME</u>
<u>SEPTEMBER 20, 2012</u>

Dah Dah DAH DAH
Dah Dah DAH DAH

Worship your name . . .	Jesus
Holy	Jesus
Righteous	Jesus
Wonderful	Jesus
Magnificent	Father
ALPHA and OMEGA	
Beginning and Ending	
Lord of Lords	
And Kings of Kings	
Exalted	Father
Holy One	
Morning Star	
Risen One	

Song like undulation, angels of fire Forward one after other
La La LaLa
La La LaLa
Lah Dah Dah Dah
Dah Dah dot Dah Dah

La La LaLa
La La LaLa
Lah Dah Dah Dah
Dah Dah dot Dah Dah

Master and Lord
Jehovah Jireh
Almighty God
Everlasting Father

Dancing Jumping, worshipping, fast pace, fast beat, dah dah dot dah dah

THE POWER OF HIS GLORY SEPTEMBER 23, 2012

(ANGELS TRAMPLING, DANCING IN WHITE ROBES, UP AND DOWN IN CIRCLE, FAST PACE)

Praise your name
Thank you Lord Jesus
Worship you
Thank you Father

Holy One
Lives forevermore
King of Kings
He is Lord Jesus

La La Lah
Da Da Da Dah Dah
La La Lahh
Da Da Da Dah Dah

Exalted One
Magnify His Name
Lord of Lords
Desire of the Ages

Praise You Lord
Lord Between the Cherubim
MIGHTY FATHER
Gracious King
La La Lah etc.

Blessed One
You are worthy
High and Lifted Up
Seated on the Throne

Bowls are passed around in Heaven
The joy of the Lord is evident

They pour them out on people of the Lord
That they might bless your name
"Oh Father"

WORSHIPPING HIM OCTOBER 2, 2012

POUND (Angels pounding their feet)
Da da da—dah lah lah la
POUND
Da da da—da da dah la la

Tinkel dah da De dell Aye Aye Aye
Tinkel dah da Da de ah mi so toe

I love you Lord
And I want you to know
You are God of all
And the Mighty One

Angels all around
In the city today
Worshiping God
In every way
Watching clouds move
In the sky so high
Joy and laughter He brings
By His Name Lifted High

YOU WON'T SEE ME UNTIL YOU LOOK FOR ME OCTOBER 23, 2012

Fire in the aisle way
Morgan Stern an empty place
Financial markets all decrepit
Stocks down
People running
Shouting
Jesus help us

Time is ending
Nobody hears my voice
They all listen
To the songs they sing
Won't last forever

When I speak
They must listen
Or they will find,
The doors will be shut

Open your hearts receive His love
Look not to the East or West
But to me
Amen

Praise His Wonderful Name for telling all of this. Halleluyah, halleluyah, Halleluyah.

I JUST WANT MORE OF YOU OCTOBER 23, 2012

I just want more of you   Da Da da Daa Dah Dah
When the candles open   Lah La Da Da La Lahhh
And people speak your name   La Lahh La La La Laahh
Then I want more of you   Da Da Da Dah Dah Dahhhh

Jesus you make me hungry   DaDa Dahhh De DeDe Dah Dah
Nothing can satisfy me   La La La Da Da Di
But your Holy Name   Da Da Dahhh Dah-Dahhhh (High end note)

I want more of you (High)   La La Lah Lah La Ooo
When storms may come   Da Da Da Dahhhh
And darkness resides   Da Dah Dah Laa
You show your Holy Will   Da Da Da Da Da Da
To break the tide   Da Da Da Da
And I want more of yourselves   La La Lah Lah Laaa

I want more of you . . . . Jesus
I want more of you . . . .
I . . . want . . . more . . . of . . . youuuuuuu

TIME'S DELAY NOVEMBER 15, 2012

A target in darkness
Evening comes
The fire's grow
Someone is calling you
Night time falls
When prayers are Answered
While Men sleep
And Women dream
Awaken by his noises
That she grows to enjoy
The music of Man's Being
The Callousness of His Ways
Much to do, Much to say,
To be ready for His Maker

Time flows-Waters to Shiloh
Ebbing, Turning, Meandering
Consummate
He hears our prayers
Now listen to me
Why don't you praise me more?
I'll Listen
Then you will be blessed

Father thank you
Amen

CLING TO ME NOVEMBER 3, 2012

The Lord helped me to write this during a time of frustration and pain as the glory through it I wanted to capture in my heart to feel the joy. And in the midst of it all Jesus heard my voice. Thank you Lord for the worship of the International House of Prayer in Kansas on November 15, 2012 at 1:49 pm. Bless the college and answer their prayers and give them peace and bless the world through that ministry Father God. In Jesus name, Amen.

Cling to me Da Da da
Cling to me Da da dahhhh
When desperation occurs you can cling to me la lalala la la la lah lahh ha lahh
It's going to be okay
When you hold on today
Then you will hear my voice
And rejoice
Believe in me
That I'll see you through
I just need you
To cling to me

I know it's not easy
When everything's wrong
Sometimes there's a difference
When you sing that song
When hurt and pain resounds
And tears are all around
I'll listen
And you will hear
Cling to me
Just cling to me (background voices-*cling to me)*
Cling to me *(cling to me)*

Praise you and thank you Father God. Thank you.
(Confirmation IHOPKC November 15, 2012, 2:06pm Teach me to lean, to cling on you) God, you are Holy.

MORE THAN YOU CAN ASK NOVEMBER 30, 2012

ECE   Slow, each word

I AM the Lord   La La La Laaa
I created thee   Da La La La Laaaa
I walk down   Da Da Daaa
Your city street   Da Da Da Dahhh

I hear your prayers
I know what you feel
When you're hurt in pain
Then I will heal

I AM your God
I know what you need
I've been there before
I know what you see

There is a name
That can make you whole
His name is Jesus
So I AM told

I know your joy
When you're upon my knee
As you bow down
And worship me

Holy, Holy
Is the Lord our God
Wonderful One
Who knows it's a hard life

Jesus
Wonderful one
Who is my King
Upon the Throne

I WANT MORE OF YOU GOD

SCIENTIFIC FORMULAS I

Calciumtrate
Collective tissue
Turn man into
A Stately Being
Island called Easter
Has material to
Change Men's souls
To seek me out
Towers of strength

ELECTROMAGNETIC

L/CW=J5-Distribution Rate Control (DRC)
$\quad$ J5-DRC x Coefficient Rate (CR)
$$\overline{}$$
Rate Of Transmission In Degrees

NUCLEAR

HOW TO PUT WATER THAT BECOMES HYDROGEN OXYGEN BOMB.
Began By Parting Red Sea
Nomenclature 11/17—equivalent rate of absorption x 15 divided by 49.
When you See this happen you won't believe it.
Matthew 9:17

AIR AND MATTER

ADOPTION RATE OF AIR AND SPACE

Ezekiel-1 Read, then listen-to Anointing Power of God, God's glory listen close. Hear the sound. What is the flow of Air in between the Cherubim Wings. That's the Absorption Rate. From then on-can solve problems-that deal with the environment. (Chapter 4).

AN EQUATION NOVEMBER 23, 2010

Differential equation
5/16 x multiple of numbers of angle 24.6 degrees
When looking at starlight by the winter's moon
Will see the arc of dominant comparisons
One will be the hemisphere of

Lucite furniture
Turn on see different colors chair-change

SEND MUSIC ACROSS SPACE

To send music across space dock part special
Eliminate matter
Requires a Regulator that . . . .
Measures clinical output of amperes
Of nocular substances emitted by the genetic signatures-
Owls use when tweaking sound measures to represent
A parallel reasoning connected by the infrastructure of the wing.
Which causes distorted wave propagation
Causing tiny cells to vibrate

(This one is different from the rest you'll see)

CLEANING OF TOXIC WASTE DUMP SITES

(FROM HIS HEAVENLY THRONE AFTER HE THROWS IT DOWN FROM HEAVEN)-It first appears as a brown stone, told for collarbone, then explained that should be a new thing then called a rivulet of white sandy paper, that unfolds and it says)

Toxic waste dumps sites
Can be cleaned up by
Earnestly desiring Chemical elements bonding
In infractional
Diamond pattern
A dish with white soap
Congealed
Producing
Arudite symbology
Cause it will feel strange and new
When applied distilled in a Portion of me

Thank you Yahweh, oh Lord thank you so much for giving this to the earth. Thank you for answering prayers.

CONTROL OF HUMAN SELF DESIRE JULY 5, 2012

RNA+Argon=causes a kinetic response.
Delineate a maxim of material life forging a bond
Causing separation to the species
A mark resemblance to a man and a woman
Selecting a design to counteract their inner urges 2 Peter 2:21

DOPPLER EFFECT JULY 5, 2012

Doppler effect
Transitional Mind Patterns of the Universe Weave
In consistent alignment with Neuro Behavior
That transcends the order of cognitive resources
Understanding the Neuro Response is key to
Making sure life remains.

FOREIGN MATTER CAUSING DISEASES JULY 5, 2012

Linear apathy consist in an atmosphere of
Quantitative analysis of foreign matter, destined
To cause diseases, mucus, alignment in lung to depreciate
The various sporas.
Sporozal of anal penetration by males of the other human sect
Avoidance is mandatory for the continuation of the human race.

WORMHOLE THEORY EXPLAINED
NOVEMBER 5, 2012

L/V4(5) or L over V4 (V Lower 4) to the Fifth Power times elemental atom substances seen by the cause and effect of dormant activities that are found in the nucleus together with the collision of dark matter concealed by the design of the Creator. You can find this in NUMBERS verse 12 Chapter 11. By this you shall know how I came to the earth in MATTHEW. Believe what I say then you shall see more, beginning tonight. Now read John before you go to bed. The Sacrifice the Lord demands is a pure heart. Read my word aloud to them, Now Go!!

Numbers 11:12 Have I conceived all this people? have I begotten them, that thou shouldest say unto me, Carry them in thy bosom, as a nursing father beareth the sucking child, unto the land which thou swarest unto their fathers?

SCIENTIFIC FORMULAS II

1. A medical marvel that would take the sting away instantly. Combined chemical, Iceland island Institution has medicine when concentrate will kill the effect of bee sting.

2. Music from Heaven resides in Music Box of Savior. To access it, have to give the key when worship. From Heavenly Spheres you will hear His voice, then song of grace. (Given to you let them out!) It happens when you seek my face. May want, can't give until I say so.

    Eat from the vine—How ministry start. Now just sleep watch what I say.

3. To Change The Hearts of men by reading My word. And giving them an ordorless substance that tobacco has, that will help them study. Needed to do it for a reason, but nobody ever came to me for it. White substance diff from rest (Chemicals) in plant. Inception, can't see it except with a microscope. Create Raleigh to give to the world. Wise men listen and increase. A formula comes to mind.

4. Eat from the vine. How ministry start. Now just sleep, Water, what in garden

SPHERICAL RADIO ELEMENT

Spherical radio element
Conclusion of Matter
Participle Principal
That 74 divided by 1.57=the Numerical Value of Colossians 3:12

NOMOID CRAFT

433 Horsepower
Slant Reverse L
Protractors
Constant Flux
Parameters Green Yellow Blue wing
Give to Jolly to finish four million
Carbon Fiber alcove
With induction center ring
That converts energy to voltage electricity
That gives cell rings a pure charge
A notable answer
Eight million launch first vessel

A WEAPON OF WARFARE

Bicycle with tracks
Instable Core
Inanimate objects disappear around it
Tracer beams fired
This is a destabilization object
Used to kill soldiers
They worked hard to prepare it
For war in the future
It will take time for people to overcome its' effects
As cells regenerate while organ tissue damage is repaired
When you pray and give honor to God they will be healed
Of their infirmity.

Thank you and praise you Father

GIVEN BY GOD ON PSALM SUNDAY 4/1/12 LIGHT EMIT FROM BLACK HOLE

RH4 The region of time that the atom splits under certain conditions
This is the formula for several points of reference where light emits
From the Black Hole.

This is in Direct Proportion To A Number Devised by
The God of Heaven

Thank you Jesus

WAVE ENERGY (ALSO ON PSALM SUNDAY)

Potential Exist through Atom Bomb to
Make Wave Energy before exhaust fossil fuels
To combine-fissionable effects while and During

DISCOVERY THROUGH THINKING (APRIL 10, 2012) ABOUT FUTURE CAR

QUOTEINT TO HELP PEOPLE LEARN ABOUT THEMSELVES

Wind Collector (every facet of the car meant to scoop wind)
Air goes through sun roof through car out front escaping outside vents
S curvature, (like ram jet) Ports in side front air escape point to tail section
Linear Hybrid Design
Pressure
Expansion Rods
Pull Alone Individuals
Pressure Systems
Mounted on Back of Motor
Take over Induction
Training System Different Than Mankind Thinking
Sleek New Virginal
Womb Safety Engine
Look like machine, I think a person
Metal not meant to go 100 mpg
But a person
Spiritual Creatures move fast
Think Man, Think Certain Formula
Maybe just words

Inept
Way Man Think
What if I had a merry life to share tell

Then became one, whose Angel knew the way
Then worship me
Listen to the voice of the Spirit
Then hear my WORD
See all Knowledge, Wisdom and Understanding
Then can move fast in the Spirit
You're thinking Man's thoughts
You think coefficient
Isn't it about me!
Hallelujah! Got it!

You look at life as one big transport system.
<u>Why Don't You Worship Me More????</u>
Angel of darkness rule city
Worship Breaks the Stronghold

<u>CURE FOR HURTING HANDS</u> October 2, 2012

Triglycerides can be used for anointing people's hands when they seem to be hurting.

WISDOM OF GOD 1

MIRACLES BY FAITH

1. "IN JESUS NAME BE HEALED!" To Say To Purify Waters Across Earth, Africa.

2. "LORD BLESS THIS FOOD AND MULTIPLY IT!" To say over food to multiply

3. "THIS CHILD OF A WOMAN'S BIRTH, LET HER BE BLESSED IN CHRIST JESUS—HOLY AND RIGHTEOUS NAME. Women Birthing rate Increase.

CHANGE HEARTS OF MAN

Change Hearts of Man by reading my word and giving them an odorless substance that tobacco has that would help them study. I needed to do it for a reason but nobody ever came to me for it. White substance, different from rest, in plant inception, can't see it except with microscope. Create Raleigh to give to world. Wise man listen and increase. A formula come to mind. Know.

MAN A MUSICAL BEING

GENESIS 6 TALKS ABOUT A MUSICAL BEING. A NOTABLE BEING HAS MUSIC INSIDE. PLEASANT TO THE EAR. DRAW IT OUT. A MUSIC BOX. HE LISTENS, HE SINGS THEN I COME UPON HIM AND PLAY A SONG THEN ALLOW HIM TO WRITE THE SONG DOWN FOR OTHERS. (*Thank you God, you are so good*)

BIRTH CONTROL CAUSES CANCER
OCTOBER 18, 2011

BIRTH CONTROL CAUSES BODY TO SHUTDOWN-PRODUCES CHEMICAL THAT CAUSES CANCER. WHY WOMEN STRAIN TO HAVE BABY CAUSE HEART ATTACK.

HEALING OF POST TRAUMATIC STRESS

POST TRAMATIC STRESS GONE
AS YOU TAKE CARE OF BUSINESS FOR THE LORD

WISDOM OF GOD 2

November 9, 2010

Worship of the Lord will destroy strongholds, darkness and evil around Russia, America, India, etc. All we have to do is worship the Lord Jesus Christ.

November 28, 2010 SUNDAY, GOD IN SERMON SPEAK "**BEING THANKFUL**"

1. Being Thankful is not just a common saying
    a. But an Attitude of the Heart
    b. Say THANK YOU LORD!!!!!!!

2. How Does It Make You Feel?
    a. Wonderment for all He has done.

3. Thankfulness is a Heart Attitude. How Cultivate?
    a. YOU LISTEN TO HIS VOICE-GIVE INSTRUCTION
    b. BE READY TO SING IN THE MORNING
    c. TELL HIM HOW GOOD HE HAS BEEN TO YOU
    d. WORSHIP HIM IN JOYFUL SONGS AND SINGING
    e. LEARN TO ACKNOWLEDGE—(YAHWEH) HIM AS LORD

THEN HE WILL BLESS YOU

THE LORD'S HEART

God was showing me something one day as I looked at others. He told me I have a different heart from my sister' heart. It was clogged up. She could see by the light of lantern beside her while I chose to remain stirring at the darkness and catching glimpse of things I knew where they should be. In conclusion the matter before the court is difference between two objects. One stationary and one on an elliptical pattern throughout the universe. You could say one in the heart department is closed while the other sheds light for many. I have built up a forceful barrier called walls of Envy, Jealousy, Anger that are hard to put down. On asking the Lord, "How I get rid of them?" He spoke, You don't!" Let me take them away by your 1) Learning to love 2) Giving until it hurts 3) Loving those that hurt you. This will alleviate the sinful desires in your flesh causing the desire to wane, to keep you happy.

1. Envy   opposite give
2. Jealousy   opposite to love
3. Anger   opposite to love those that hurt you

"This is my heart," says the Lord.

FEBRUARY 4, 2010

Lord speak "Cloud of smoke, Tanks coming, They have a Strategy."

APRIL 19, 2010

BEGAN AT SHEPERD'S GRACE CHURCH
START A MINISTRY-SISTERS OF FIRE
They have to know me first

Then I can use themselves
Make them happy
Have true life
Then when the time is right
Marriage will come
But you must remember
It is not a casual thing
To tell a woman that life will be better.
It must be shown to her
In the scriptures
She must know-all she is giving up.
Shall return to her ten-fold

MAY 31, 2010

BEGAN AT SHEPHERD'S GRACE CHURCH (FINANCIAL STRATEGY)
Broadmine and Going
Helix
Pattern Initiate
    2   Circles
1.   Financial Goal Setting
2.   Collect debts
3.   Financial Gain
4.   Income Debt Restructure
5.   Collective Bargaining Agreements

APRIL 11, 2012

BEGAN AT SHEPHERD'S GRACE CHURCH (MEN A PLACE TO PRAY)

Start a medium (Neighbor)Hood for servants of God
Worship center
None but the Lord
Million men come
Call it **JEHOVAH THE LORD**!

Circular Institute in ARCHEITECT
Read, Study and Prayer
Seek advise from the Lord
Remember to build it in a round circle
That men might come and worship God
Start in Georgia, Atlanta
A million men over time
Building 44,000 square feet
Has Gymnasium, kitchen eat,
Storage Below
Chairs & Desk in rooms
Place to rest outside
Two Jeeps

JULY 18, 2011
LORD SPEAKING ABOUT RALEIGH

THE PROBLEM IN THIS CITY IS THAT THEY LIKE HAVING A MAN AROUND THEM.

WHAT TO DO TO MAKE THEM SEE YOU?

1. TELL THEM I LOVE THEM
2. MAKE THEM SEE ME MORE KINDLY AS A SAVIOR WHO CARES
3. TELL THEM I SEE THEIR TEARS
4. I FEEL THEIR PAIN
5. I NEED THEM TO SEE HOW GOOD I AM
6. THAT THEY CAN RETURN TO ME NO STRINGS ATTACHED AND FEEL GOOD AGAIN

REASON

REASONING FACTORS
ARE CALL CENTERS IN THE BRAIN
THAT MUST BE ANALYZED TO UNDERSTAND WHICH WAY
DEVELOPMENT IS BEGINNING IN CHILD
THERE CAN BE AN ABSENCE OF CONCENTRATION CAUSED
BY KEEPING ONESELF IN A PARANOID STATE ALL THE TIME
CHILDREN NEED TO GET OUTSIDE
WHERE THEY CAN BE HEALED
BY THE CREATED JOY THAT SURROUNDS THEM
MANY ARE LACKING THE ESSENTIAL ELEMENTS
TO GIVE THEM THEIR ANSWERS TO PRAYER
TO ALLOW GOD TO WORK WITH THEIR MINDS IN A
SUPERNATURAL WAY
TO GIVE THEM A LIFE OF PURE JOY

IT'S LIKE A MAN WALKING BY A CHAMBER DOOR

JUST SAY HI

YOU NEED TO SAY HI, SPEAK TO PEOPLE, ASK HOW THEY ARE
DOING?
THIS WILL LEAD TO PEOPLE TELLING AND AN OPENING TO
GIVE THE GOSPEL
INSANITY THAT'S WHERE MOST OF THESE KIDS ARE HEADED
TO—THEY NEED-JUST TO HAVE SOMEONE TO TALK TO IS
THE KEY
ABSENCE OF PARENTS IS A VITAL KEY-THAT'S WHY IN CHURCH
SHOULD HAVE A PROGRAM THAT ALLOWS KIDS TO TALK

TO OLDER ADULTS ONE ON ONE, THEN THEY CAN HEAR CHOICES THAT CAN CHANGE THEIR EXISTENCE WITHOUT FEELING NOONE'S LISTENING

CHEMICAL ANALYSIS DATA IS BETTER IF THEY CAN TALK TO SOMEONE

IN TIME FOR MAJOR GROWTH

1) LOOK IN GOD'S WORD
2) WRITE DOWN THINGS APPLICABLE LEARN AND
3) WALK IN THEM

WORSHIP YOUR NAME LORD THANK YOU FOR ALL THE WISDOM, UNDERSTANDING AND KNOWLEDGE THAT HAS COME FOR YOUR WILL TO BE KNOWN ON THE EARTH. PRAISE YOU AND THANK YOU LORD. ALMIGHTY GOD, EVERLASTING FATHER, PRINCE OF PEACE.

PRAYER TIME FOR ALL MILITARY FAMILIES TO WORSHIP JESUS

1. START PRAYING FOR HUSBAND OR WIFE
2. WHOLE MILITARY
3. COUNTRY
4. NATION
5. WORLD-MILITARIES AROUND THE WORLD
6. ANGELS LOOSED IN MILITARY CAMPAIGNS
7. HEART OF GOD IN SOLDIERS
8. JESUS GIVE PEACEFULNESS
9. RESTORATION OF NATION, FAMILY
10. PRESIDENTIAL GRACES-TO LIVE AT PEACEFULNESS
11. REVIVAL IN ISRAEL-GLOBAL
12. FIRE OF GOD SET IN ALL HEARTS
13. KNOWLEDGE OF HIS WORDS FILL THE EARTH
14. PROPENSITY TO GO AND MAKE DISCIPLES OF MEN
15. DISCIPLESHIP COURSES FOR WIVES IN THE MILITARY (WITH FAMILY-OTHER WOMEN, SOLDIERS THEY MEET-ENCOURAGING THE WOMEN TO BE STRONG FOR THE LORD, RAISE UP A GENERATION OF MEN THAT LOVE GOD AND DAUGHTERS THAT WORSHIP AT HIS THRONE OF GLORY)
16 THIS WILL BRING PEACE TO THE NATION

HOLIDAY OF GOD

While they do their holiday we do ours (Holiday for Christians and Jews) 40 days-called

THE ISRAELI GOD AND HIS MESSIAH

FOR CHRISTIANS THE WORSHIP OF YAHSHUA, THE LORD JESUS CHRIST

FOR JEWS THE WORSHIP OF THE GOD OF ISRAEL & MESSIAH.

1. HOW? NIGHTLY NO DINNER
2. SINGING
3. HOLD HANDS PRAYING
4. SEEK MY FACE
5. REPENTING
6. CALLING ON MY NAME ASKING ME

GOD WILL GIVE THEM DIVINE CURES IN THE BODY IF THEY ASK HIM IN A CERTAIN WAY.

FATHER GOD of our LORD JESUS CHRIST *please look down upon us and heal our bodies. We wish to thank you for every blessing you have given dear Father. And we give you all the glory in Jesus Christ Holy name.*

SONG TO BE SUNG on days of worship

GOD I NEED YOU

Lord you are one
Every day I seek you
When the dawn breaks
Multiple mercies fall on me
As I stand before you now
Oh Oh Maker of Heaven
Rejoicing before your throne
In adoration, kneeling at your feet
You are Jehovah Jireh, my provider
My Righteousness

Angels surround thee
When we look to Heaven and sing
You are my all, you are my everything

I need you Lord Jesus

NOVEMBER 3, 2011 WAITING ON THE LORD, GAVE ME WORD LOOK UP

(Question about working with the homeless)

Humble yourselves in the sight of the Lord, and he shall lift you up. James 4:10

Render to Caesar the things that are Caesar's and to God the things that are God's. Mark 12:17

WHAT CAN BE DONE TO HELP THEM COME BACK TO ME?

1. Repent
2. Believe the Gospel
3. Sexually Immoral Behavior-must be displaced with a love for Christ
4. Lewdness and Subjection to Money, Going over to idolatry-instead become serious worshipers of the Lord Jesus Christ.

Let Jesus be our Lord and Savior then will have joy and peace throughout nation, diseases gone. Men and women married to each other, children blessed-grow in skill, knowledge increase, money flow throughout land.

TO THE ONE IN THE CULT OF THE BUILDERS WHO NEED JESUS

"Tell them I am who I said I AM!"

ARMOURBEARER

THINGS YOU WILL HAVE TO KNOW TO BE AN ARMOURBEARER IN YOUR CITY AND MINISTRY IN DOWNTOWN YOUR CITY.

1. MORNING PREPARATION—I will enter his gates with thanksgiving in my heart, I will enter His courts with praise.
A. WORSHIP OF GOD–Read Word, Praise Him, Sing, Dance, While in worship singing or laying before him quietly, if God gives you a word listen and write down what he says.
B. HEART ATTITUDE-Forgive anyone that has hurt you, even family, keep short accounts of what others have done to you, Cast down all vain

imaginations, Focus on God be clear in the thought processes. Never be worried about how God used you yesterday or what he's going to do today or your sermon. Relax, enjoy nature, open your mouth and he will fill it.

C. Going downtown you will need a bible, a sheet of paper, an ink pen-(write addresses if someone wants you to be in contact) a hat for the sun and winter cold. An umbrella, Rain and summer heat, winter gloves and an parking space. Something to drink makes the throat easier-water, etc.

D. 1. When you get to the courthouse pray and ask God to come be a part, for His glory, not by might or power but by my spirit sayeth the Lord.

* Ask God to open their ears to hear, stop anything capturing their attention. He will give you prayers to say.
* Anoint place pray over it
* Let God lead
* Sing Songs/worship praise
* Read a Psalm
* When God speak-(or if he told you night before) go to scriptures and read word he gives you. Then as he tells you, explain the scripture, how it affects their lives today.
* Use examples God gives (you may see a man carrying His son, if you are speaking that God wants them by His side. Speak, like a man holding a little boy by his side, is the way God wants us to be with him).
* Let them know he's coming soon and about hell if they decide not to
* Give altar call-ask if anyone want Jesus
* Bless the hearers May the grace and peace be upon all who hear
* If someone comes by the bench or is sitting and listening ask if they need prayer, then before pray ask if they are saved. If not lead into how to be saved and sinners prayer.

2. While you minister

* It is good to be in twos, one passing out tracts and praying for the other or taking aside those who want to interrupt.
* Some will come up to disturb from the devil-wanting to argue, asking for money, asking about cigarettes, telling what they know of the bible,

wanting to talk, ask questions about the city. Usually I speak let me finish first, or wave to acknowledge them and only if the Lord convicts or tells me to stop and answer will I ask. (It's important to note mainly we are there to give the gospel and Lift up Christ-our mission is to those who God is sending to receive the words of life).

- Young police may come not use to ministers, old ones know-may say have to move down a few feet. Pray for them
- Some will come to read after you or to talk about the bible and if God sends a helper it is well or an exhorter. But know those who labor among you. Is this sound doctrine, is this person born again, mature in the faith or do they just want to showboat and be seen? This is the ministry God has given to you, watch who you allow in the pulpit.
- People will be passing by, some will look, some will hurry by and rush not to hear, others will act like they don't hear. But give the word-it will not come back void. Different parts of what you speak are for different people passing by. Don't be afraid of their faces. Know that angels are around you to protect you and the Holy Ghost is there surrounding like on the day of Pentecost. Those that make comments, "I don't believe that" and are walking, just say "May the Lord bless you"
- After you give a word that God wants you to never worry if it was good enough. It was and God will use it for it's expected end-somebody will get blessed and later tell you.
- People will pass by an encourage you, saying keep it up, etc.
- When you minister God will bless you that day afterwards and while you are doing it. People give food, you might see a friend you haven't seen in years, God tells you the next step in ministry. You will meet ministers you may work with in the future. God will confirm word, you will hear part of what you preach later the same day on radio, supermarket-somewhere.
- God may tell you to speak louder, tell you he is pleased afterwards, in the morning he may tell you go downtown and preach that day. God may warn you about what to expect and people you will meet that day.
- Angels with, you will feel God's power go out as preach and after. You will feel a change in the city.
- People will try to praise you, saying good word etc. Simply tell them **"All glory to God"**-so He will get the glory and we will not be puffed up then buffeted to pop our big heads.

<u>Last Things</u>

3) Parting words:

Tell them the Lord is coming soon as you close, explain. ie As the state fair is coming closer and you prepare for it, don't forget the Lord is coming soon, prepare.

4) Give them a Benediction:

May the Lord bless them that believe on His name. (It is not good just to ask the Lord to bless everyone in your city because some are in sin and we do not want to bless sin) however if you add "May he bless-all who call on His name" or All who heard His word today and believe.

5) Answer questions to any sitting near that ask about the bible:

When the Holy Ghost gives you an utterance ask the Lord to bless the city, nation and globe.

6) Worship God on the way home. Singing hymns and Christian songs will restrengthen your inner woman.

2 hours of prayer for every hour of sermon helps

DECLARE, DEMAND WITHOUT DOUBT

<u>THE LORD (WORSHIP HIS NAME)</u>
<u>NOVEMBER 4, 2012</u>

An early morning vision, the vision came while in deep sleep. Jesus was there at a dinner table, His eyes were elaborate. He spoke a command, directing me to Feed Him. (instead of Him feeding me as was supposed). He in His love, peace, beauty spoke to me to feed Him, I picked up the spoon and desired to bring it to His lips.

WORSHIP THE LORD HOLY, HOLY, HOLY
NOVEMBER 12, 2012

Before I woke, I had a vision in sleep worshiping. There were several of us around a space putting (like) chess pieces in four directions like in Ezekiel the cherubim, then with four more pieces with wings to conclude the piece Cherubim. Then concluding the piece it looked like the seen from Revelations 4. All white pieces, then the worship coming from us as Holy, Holy, Holy came out of our mouths, from our souls. In heart knew as later the Spirit spoke be "Holy and Righteous."

""The angels around you were the pieces, you were off track and I was showing you how to get back on track through worshiping "Holy, Holy, Holy."

Thank you Father. "Holy Is the Lord!" You are Jesus." "There is none like you, Angels bow before you." I Am an Angel of God telling you what to do . . . Remember He is Lord and needs the worship to make you whole. Angels are here now . . . rest.

(THE COLLECTIVE THREE)
QUEEN BEE

The hive was buzzing as his grandfather moved it and its queen from a tree on a crowded street. It would mean more honey for their business. His family was successful in the honey making business in the 50's, 60's, 70's and 80's and when he took over in the nineties out of college with his MBA, the 90's. He made huge use of marketing and the internet to push their products and his wife's international legal skills to protect their burgeoning enterprise as they gobbled up other small beekeepers. She was two years his senior but couldn't help but being enticed by him when she heard about the enterprise. She was extremely beautiful, with a potent legal mind and deadly as after they diversified into many bee products, she made sure their rights where not infringed upon. He, his wife and family where all billionaires by 1999 with a product line headed to more expansion during the dot com burst. His lowering prices saved them as they gained more grocery shelf and new customers with their first sampler packages. Gloria, his wife's passion was traveling to Africa and helping third world countries, and the women in them start businesses along with spreading the gospel. She just loved traveling. He loved researching and learning more about honey bees, the queen bee and the hive. The global knowledge was ready for him to use just before the Tower Tragedy when he was getting different varieties of honey in a special kit and learning to fight the African Bee. They were known low key as they didn't keep a high profile and rarely entertained or went out preferring their own chef, dining doing business, talking and conferring as their daughters listened and put in their own acumen. His wife was on her second passion helping African American women across the United States and being on endless committees, visiting the White House etc. when he lost her and his daughters during the tragedy as she was having breakfast talking to Wall street consultants and the government about the growing honey market demand and her husband's stake in it. There were odd fluctuations that where trying to come to terms with as they looked into the culprits causing it. She was having breakfast in the towers when the airliner hit and he remembered trying to call her but getting no answer and watch helplessly as he tried to get to NY. She had wanted her wedding, wedding guests and wedding night to be immaculate as they paid seven million for the ceremony and it was perfect until halfway through the wedding night. He was asleep after extensive coupling and she up sitting in the bed thinking then leaning to the dresser to get a bible and finding an old drab thing and immediately sounding her disgust. He woke as she explained the matter, citing how terrible as he called a Christian bookstore desiring to see and purchase all their top leather bound bibles and to be brought up on a cart. He soothed her with more coupling until they arrived with more room service and he had her pick until she was satisfied and he put the others and the offender out in the hallway and came back to lay on her lap as she read to him. She still felt it didn't connect with her African Female-Centerness and there wasn't one until he promised he would give thirty percent of their income until they created one. She said 75% citing she had did some things in the past and hoped God wouldn't look at repercussions and at his surprise saying they already had a billion they couldn't spend it all. He agreed with her returning to rest as she suddenly began to think about what personnel to put on a committee to form it. The rest of their honeymoon went like that as she was inspired and on the phone when they weren't off having fun. She didn't stop the next several years and putting together a secure compartmental organization to produce the work. She added to the beautiful scripted and photo immersed text 1) a Hebrew-African new language composed of all the African languages to subliminally draw each segment of the African society 2) subliminal text on how to be a positive black woman and dealing with issues of marriage, family, self, society, friendships, spiritual calling, life with Christ etc. and 3) A Hebrew bible code that shifted to the DNA of the person reading to give them Spiritual wisdom, knowledge and understanding about their situations, human interactions etc. She had learned about the subliminal use through friends high in the government that slipped her top secret information. The cover had to be of a material that when touched brought comfort and acceptance to all African women and they found it by much research then also a touch screen visual audio inside the cover of maps and materials presented. The smell of the binding had to be aroma pleasing. 200 women she formed in a collective to work. Over the years she also saw the need in the future for a strong internet presence that all African women could link up to for information, study and friend groups. This also led to the financing of a website for the future, TV, web-cast, radio, blogs, magazines, for easier access to support the bible and allow it to be an inter-phase and connecting point for all women. It was an ambitious project with all the particulars coming together seamlessly on water and stain resistant glossy white pages that hid all the Hebrew and subliminal texts and symbols combined on the paper (allowing it to look like a regular page but inputting knowledge). He put billions in an account for its marketing watching the project secretly for four years. The only disturbance was that some of the women he was told by a project supervisor were considering how they could use the change it would cause to dominate men and their children, and she advised him that he should began such a bible for men and young people. He took the advisement and reached out to his sources in Brussels, Germany, NASA etc., who had helped edit, clean, collate and rewrite the whole bible and subliminal parts into a united whole to again solicit illegal time on the massive Intel thinking supercomputers unseen in all the world. The researching, knowledge, subliminal thought and marketing to the African male took the most time as he had to be sure who he could trust and the research had to be verifiable many times as with the African young people. He considered himself blessed by God running six months behind with the Men's bible after four years and readying it for press and marketing in various media formats, electronic, ink, internet etc. The scope of the cost for producing hundreds of millions was astronomical plus the marketing campaign and he was glad the new honey products: liquid white honey for coffee and replacement for all sugar products, vitamin infused honey that hit the market in clear pellets then used everywhere and a special honey for tea (that just about took over England and the tea drinking world) kept him super profitable during the publishing stage. His institute that studied all production stages of honey and spent off companies to a) help honey growers, b) teaching world growth through planting around the world for pollination and increase beekeeping c) to remove beehives causing hazards around the world to bee facilities where they became more containable to make outputs of honey d) teaching smaller species of bees to give off scents to deter take-over of their community by the more aggressive African bee and other predators and fighting disease by herbal additives. His companies' product line had increased and he was looking at subcontracting in kiosks in malls and plazas across the globe or through minority agents in communities across the globe (like Mary Kay). The profits to his family business sustained him enough for the launch May 1, 2004 aimed at the graduation and female summer reading market with the bible worth $200.00 sold for just $10.00 at what was called an introductory offer. Then it happened, after selling 5 million initially, African women began to understand the truth and love themselves enough to be what God wanted them to be. When the positivity affected their lives others where led en-masse and the women began coming together for change as the bible was downloaded, ordered, shared and pulled off bookshelves. What had started in America went global in the second phase as it hit Europe, the African continent etc. The bible hunger added up to billions that where sold and women began to protests injustices, dropped negative influences, food, drinks, television shows etc. and worked toward helping others, their family, themselves and the African society. Companies went out of business as they stopped buying, loans where paid back, businesses where started, talents where drawn upon never used, communities of women encouraging over the internet where started, cults fell apart as masses of women finally saw the untruth, pastors lost positions or where held more accountable to be holy unto God presenting the gospel and their lifestyle without compromise or shadow of variance, politicians lost positions, standards where higher for their predecessors and leaders of communities where dismissed or made to move forward in helping the people. The world was set on its' head by the change, higher standards and Christian beliefs of a conglomerate of African women working together to glorify God in all their choices. African males where made to move in force with the African women' new thought, change of thinking and collectively moving. This affected the market in changes of living, billions in spending going back into the community or betterment of life and support for the poor. The upsurge in positive change in the Female African Life by the Female Bible was happening at such a faster rate than anticipated that timely he had to release the men' Bible in a provocative campaign September 1, 2004. The campaign was to be in time for back to school and to buy dad a present the new bible for $15.00 since dad's didn't usually get anything new. The Institute Company filled all 250 million orders the first five days until it boomed. Their second commercial was of Dad's that had bought their own but received a second to give one away or send one to Africa. It boomed. The upsurge caused in two years the price of living to increase 10 percent in Africa and 2 percent around the world and in five years 25% in Africa and 8% around the world as Africans gave to help other depressed countries around the world and God blessed them as 78% of the country learned to worship Yahweh, Yahshua the Messiah and sent torrential rains, fertile soil a new nutrient based additive to a continental manure collection allowing field and the continent to be more fertile. God showed him gravity mining which gathered minerals out of the earth and left the residue on a condition they pray before and after the mining for God to restore the land and thanked him for his abundant blessing. African nations in four years had gotten rid of dictators and rulers, put a plan in place how the government and each individuals money was spent 50% to family, 40% to God and poorer nations, then 10% for self. The nations themselves in tax collecting were to give 10 percent in tithes to poorer nations. This gave them also a continental coffee market that was burnishing and bristling and on the toes to rival the world markets. By 2007 huge factories where built for exporting products and materials and in 2008 the continental finances (dollars of each country) where given the same value and backed by gold and silver. This allowed them to pay back all their debts in 2009 by gravity oil drilling on land and in the oceans around the continent and rising economically. They rivaled Japan's growth at an exponential rate causing fear on the world markets becoming the next superpower (However concerned more about the social status of its' people than technological over excess). In 2009 medical dental hospitals, universities, schooling systems, road infrastructure, housing, clean water wells, eradication of diseases, deadly pests, and abundant grow where the major concerns and budget allowances of the Continent that spent it's trillions internally with its other trillions in tithes and offerings going to help the poor in countries of the world across it's ocean and special concerns for the hurting in Israel. Providing food for the continent and sustainable lifestyle of its' inhabitants took up most of the finances during the recession (economic collapse around the world) and Africa still depended on his gravity drill company outlawed in many other nations across the world, his input, intel and finances in the coffee market and continental honey export and buying. His non-profit to help bring medicines to the continent needed in the new hospitals, clinics etc., where greatly needed until the trumpet sounding to worship God at sunrise and sunset across the continent began. As the worship began favor from God began. Night rains began and knowledge of plants began coming to people and children that collectively was gathered to spread across the continent and grow medicinal herbs and plants en-masse. Godly knowledge wisdom and discernment had begun when the first Women's bible was opened and since then knowledge of Africans superseded the expectation of their peers. It was said in any business meeting be sure to have an African or African descendant to dissect and give new input. The foundational thesis held in quantum fields of occupation as new ideas, more efficient production came from the creative logical minds enhanced by the study of God's word and their souls taking in Hebraic, DNA, subliminal thought, allowing their spirits to be more in control. His people were leaders, teaching the rest of the world to catch up. He had thought the advantage in time would have him making bibles for other cultures, but they were learning from his people (the various cultures) and excelling themselves. His company however was beginning to suffer a wound he couldn't stop. Competitors had now entered the honey market with heavy financiers and a vast array of knockoffs of his products. He was ready for the power seven he had intel of but the other minor seven he didn't see raising their heads until the first of the year which disrupted his plans. Countries of the world where beginning to kick his company out of their bee and honey production that used him extensively before and certain unpopulated islands he used or rented for honey making and pollinating where suddenly snatched back and given to his competitors as deals where made back door. Globally his company was taking a hit and at home in the US as the government decided to end all honey contracts with his company and give them to the start-ups to help kick start the economy. That took away a 5 percent of his business and brought gossip on Wall-street about the private company failing from taking so many hits and the eager competition. This caused a fear then demand for honey products as the honey prices shot up, more star—ups and food companies jumped in the market and his suppliers and beekeepers demanded more finances and finally after thirteen years holding market prices down and at a low he had to increase prices in January of 2009 to stay alive. This brought rancor from the public, a portion of his customer base jumping ship which he could tell outside forces wanted all the time. They wanted to destroy his company for being competitive for so long and becoming a global powerhouse with the highest paid honey workforce and a numerous workers. His family was concerned and wanted to go public but he spoke the wound had not reached arterial flow yet and the market would come down from its saturation point after the first quarter. February held steady as he had to make more concessions to regain honey contracts smaller companies couldn't handle, or in hazardous situations or in quick work the government outsourced them to and their expertise across the world. It was only 1 % but staunched the flow a little bit. In concession he had to 1) hire 20,000 new workers, Open his multilevel minority honey associate program to 20, 000 non—minority associates 3) give up his rights to the patent of liquid white honey opening the market to all and they would throw him new government, state and global work to bring revenue back up to 2%. He was against it but his family still feeling they had a substantial lead in the selling of the liquid white honey wanted the contracts. The next week they announce a plush employee retirement program with a one million dollar deal and 20, 000 retired immediately and in a move he didn't hope for a portion went to work for his competitors. His company also announced the opening of the multilevel business to 20,000 which rankled many of his people and caused a lost in brand loyalty for a few days and then the patent suspended indefinitely for liquid white honey. Wall-street buzzed after that, honey companies jumped immediately in liquid white sales they had been holding back and where more aggressive in the market rivaling their hold product line. That's when he began to see the arterial flow at the end of the first quarter and knew without a miracle of God they would have to go public in a market already teaming with competition. He was stressed each day mostly from family, execs and company Intel. His only hope was the ten Air Foil gravity supertankers he was having built in Japan. However they were holding them even after completion until he paid the rest of the 2 billion for them. He had gone to banks and lending institutions but everyone closed their doors to him in a global conspiracy as he presented calmness in the face of high stress as he boarded the company jet that now was becoming a luxury. He had to make a decision soon as the losses where just touching on unacceptable and he thought at his corporate desk and prayed considering meeting with African countries already tight with finances keeping a crucial trade balance buying US Steel for wells. The ships with gravity mining where made to mind the ocean as it displaced water like a hydrofoil and in bay doors, open to receive minerals as it put back residue. He had a dream of Titanium in the sea and knew where to mine it, he just needed the ships. It was late after five, his family had called after the market and business reports and they wanted a meeting. His secretary then brought in the mail and correspondence and placed a letter from a law firm concerning the trial of sultry singer who had been on top the last ten years. She was the flavor of the decade, Hawaiian, sensuous, every man's dream and a beautiful soul singer who had taken over the market with her gyrations, scanty clad videos, and a haunting persona that made men and Cd buyers want her more. He went to a dinner one night at a nice club and she was there with her entourage and fans which he didn't expect. On seeing him she began to growl and he told everyone who was not filled with Jesus to leave. The place emptied quickly as the entity in her manifested and he bound it and gave Kalani a chance to speak and asked if she wanted to receive Jesus as her Savior and Lord, She said a prayer asked Christ in and confessed her sins and told all the foul spirits possessing her to go in Jesus Christ Holy name. There were shouts and things breaking as they left and her manager immediately came at him for changing her. He bound the evil spirits in the man in Christ Jesus name and asked if he wanted to be delivered, knowing the fate of the ungodly and how his tormenters would treat him. He still said no, telling them she could not get out of her contract and they would sue her if she didn't go on tour and many other threats as he yelled for them to come back and release him. He got her to his car and drove off before releasing her former manager of the heavenly hosts binding him. He had someone bug his hotel room, car when he left it and a place at the bar of his hotel. He then took Kalini to a private retreat for christian women and pastors wives on a secluded island in the Pacific ocean for her to be nourished, taught and discipled. The manager had spoken about her demise and how much she would bring in. His new law team, a hungry young firm ready to make a name. It was enough to excuse her from being at any court appearance as the judge looked seriously at the death threat. He paid the firm 100 million for her legal fees for them to push back the date of her trial and to work with spies inside the opposing legal team and an accountant who wanted a Rembrandt for his troubles. Daniel got it and heard he broke the dam and exposed the music studio and it's manipulation and stealing of her finances, time, energy, vacation etc. The up-shod was all the studio heads and top employees where put on trial for their part in abusing her financially, physically (even before eighteen years old). She was awarded 2.5 billion, control of her music, her contract and 3 record deal finished as the company was found to have albums ready in case of Kalani's demise which they had planned at the conclusion of the trial. Kalani was told he had provided for her all this time and his company was now taking a hit, so she sent an envelope by a lawyer

It was there on his desk and as he opened it he saw a check for transfer funds of 2 billion dollars and he tearfully thanked God then straightening himself transferred the amount to the Japanese and heard his ships being released from the docks. He rested before dinner with Kalani and was shown a dream of oil spills and pressure from the earth that needed to be relieved by oil drilling or gravity drilling. He woke and ordered ten more special tankers from a competitor of the Japanese for a billion in collateral as he readied to meet Kalani knowing from the last part of the dream she would be his wife that night. It all worked perfectly, the conversation, the flowers that she loved, the music in the background in the dream and the first kiss. Only a call to a pastor friend interrupted their growing emotions as they vowed before God before they continued. She was different, changed, quieter, just as sexy but reserved with a wisdom from the knowledge of God in her life. She wanted a protector to take away all the negatives in her life and just her own studio to promote her new Jewish and Messianic Jewish music and concerts. She didn't care about the rest of the money giving it to him for the tankers asking only he allow her a career and to tell him when she displeased him. He could tell that wasn't going to happen very often. She also wanted to help support the female, male and young people's bibles going into India. A fire that had burned slowly suddenly ignited in India as the bibles where hungered for and worship of false gods and odd religions declined with a hunger for Jesus Christ across the continent that couldn't be stopped.

The gravity ships came just in time as minerals taken from the ocean 24/7 supported the economy of the African continent, kept his company afloat just in the red even as 75% of his beekeeping subcontractors formed their own company and increased the cost of his supply and kept the bibles flowing into India, Turkey etc., as demand increased dramatically. In 2010 the over saturated honey market finally dropped over night after January 1st and sent sellers tumbling and suddenly every one scrambling to get out of it. He ordered six gravity oil tankers immediately on line as he pushed the finish offering another half billion and had them gravity drilling at sites to take pressure off the earth. Then he began to buy up, merge and make new contract with bee associations and global bee companies. He was in the drivers seat and it cost him as the prices continually plunged and every one wanted to do business as he bought up interests getting loans from banks at enormous sums as they hoped his family would fall. It took till the end of January for the honey market to stable and the end of March until he could pay all his creditors two-thirds of what he owed them to their astonishment. It helped that he was able to monopolize in the Russian and Chinese markets and was supplying assistance and support to increase their crop yield 100 percent. The oil prices remaining high had helped him as he kept the tankers sea drilling and cleaning up oil spills. Kalani started her long awaited concert touring as people wondered about her new videos, music and Jewish dancing ready to rock at her concerts again. Her witness formulating Jesus stole the headlines as the world did a double take and her Christian website linked to the Bibles became ultra-popular. The African economy rose and quality of life as gravity roads where put in, manure increase fertile fields as African scientist made waste production centers more efficient using animal and human fertilizer, gravity drilling increased irrigation, and he was led to buy large qualities of free range livestock for farmers and families in every nation on the African continent. America wanted to be his biggest provider as he stipulated no steroids, drugs etc and in exchange he also got help in knowledge of others trying to make subliminal bibles or distorted teaching to draw many from the African female and male bibles. He had teams that went in to ensure they never got to the market and counteracted negative forces coming at his work by sometimes huge organizations. He squeezed every ounce out of his ships and tankers nightly doing quick turnarounds and finding troves of the most precious metals that he usually told them from dreams in his sleep. In May an oil sea platform exploded causing an huge oil spill in the US. Someone in the government immediately said they needed his help and the government and British oil company responsible immediately finished the payment of the new tankers in exchange for the 16 tankers gravity pumping the oil. His family exposed the business in a news magazine being on the cover to push him to sell the business. The exposure he didn't want as they said he owned thirty five percent of the stock and a ruling majority and called the shots to make them one of the top Wall-street business and they gloated. Many would become envious he knew and their Golden Age would be over as they had insulted and boasted unwittingly against the powers that be behind Wall-street. Their decline was inevitable, he took no calls as he was followed by the press and media and people came from everywhere to meet him. He had someone investigate who was behind all this and found that the government wanted to make a deal with his family for the company and giving them 2 small fortune 500 companies each for their shares then raid or buy him out. It was all conditioned on them reaching a stock owner who could tip the balance with his ten percent before he met with him. Daniel had been anticipating this and had the meeting set up. The next morning he was told his secretary had canceled his meeting and set up one with the client instead. He fired her and locked her out from any company intel as he tried to make the meeting. He saw them shaking hands and walking out below him and was about to interrupt before his sister behind him said Kalani is on the phone (more of a threat). After the call which was mostly about the beach and a shoot, his siblings then demanded control of the company as majority holders. He asked if they all were in on it and consented as they said they were for various reasons, saying he wasn't sane enough and they were greedy. He spoke about what would happen to their family company, the employees and how they would lose with their new companies even uniting together. They laughed, called him a fool and then held a gun again and said they would pay him and wanted to buy out the rest of his share. He understood that they had gotten finance through the Banks of China but told them no. He said he had to think about it. They wanted to reason with him but he said he would need another day, besides it all had to clear. They trusted him after he gave them his word and it gave him a day to warn all his top people, staff and employees to leave the company, look for other jobs and take the one million dollar departure package offered them as soon as they where asked. The next day he got behind the scenes and found out the government wanted the company on the cheap to pay back part of the loan to China as it would give them a monopoly stake in the global honey production world market and a way to spy out other countries deficiencies. An account was set up the next day with seven billion for his shares and a request he stay on as the top executive until another CEO became acquainted with the company. She came impressive with twelve of her Chinese managers as she looked over the company, picked it apart and spoke about where it would go in less than an hour. She wanted codes changed and he effectively locked out as they would be taking over. When the discussion were over they left as quickly as they came as did his siblings desiring to entertain the new CEO. He was left at the table with the government people who where telling him they had a little problem with the 7 billion going through and while they waited perhaps they could interest him in a few companies. He told them he wasn't really interested but they asked him to look anyway. He told them he had to check with his researchers and would get back with them the next day by which time he suggested the check had better been cleared. How about dinner the beautiful government female said, I've already made reservations she said and would have someone pick him up. His researchers told him the best choices to make of the fortune companies, but he wasn't thrilled over most of them all. A car arrived with the beautiful agent inside as he asked where her cohort was. "Some things, are not needed," she said and handed him a small drive for his PC. He pulled up several companies, one that had a cure for malaria in its vaults, another that had a cure for diabetes and a third that had a substitute chocolate material that could stabilize low and high blood pressure with a stable diet. She then showed him on another file 200 drill sites he had not accessed or thought of and the knowledge several people where investigating the gravity tankers and a news article about to come out and several magazine articles with a book on the way. She told him she was really Israeli and that she also wanted him to ask for a fourth company, a crown jewel in the midst of bankruptcy with the government. This fourth company was tied up with the military and in its' vault the prototype for a robotic soldier, with 11 inch armor, laser and solar weapons, controlled remotely and as fast and stealth as a cougar. They would need a million very soon and storage facilities in Israel where being prepared and underground test sites. The production would need the 5 billion after he initially gave the government 2 billion for the four businesses. A portion of the five billion would also be used to prop up the Israeli economy since it had been taking a lot of hits lately and its resources where draining. She hoped also he would provide financial help from the mining as the burgeoning African economy was also cutting in their trade businesses. He asked how he knew she was Israeli as she then told the driver to take them to the restaurant and she allowed him to call one of his people to check. She was clear by the time they left the limousine and returned to her tight bean counter face taking no prisoners when he met her again after she changed with her coworker. Reilly the male agent was surprised when he didn't desire any on the lists and named his own and at their less expensive prices he could only push for 2 billion out of the 7 billion assuring him they wouldn't look in the vaults and every patent was his. Reilly simply said at the conclusion of the meeting five billion was a lot of money, perhaps they could do business in another week and had Millisence show him a second file. I'll look over it. You do that he said, taking Millisence away. She returned the next morning as they had quite an expensive breakfast as she outlined after he gravity mined what materials they would need for production and quick trade for cash. She was working on pumping up a trillion as the arterial flow in their economy was bigger than she thought and they had people closing off the arteries. She closed her PC, spoke about the meal being excellent and hoped they would meet again. She went out breezily like the evening air leaving a lingering scent that never seemed to end after it quietly faded moments before. He was walking easily with that thought until he got out in the cool wind and felt a chill. Something somewhere was happening in the darkness and he had to find out what it was. He went to his office and made calls and combed over everything, calling his people and checking on the status of the subliminal bible for all the other 3 races, Asia, Anglo-Saxon and Hispanic. They were finish with a half billion in the production mode in island storage and that's where he felt the nudge in his spirit. He checked about dark copies, most of them halted and delayed until someone thought they heard something and he jumped on it. He didn't get the answer to the next day of a student doing the shooting at a high school and a book like the bible being found in his material. He had someone pick it up and was lucky one of the policeman had studied the subliminal bible and recognize the difference in the dark one that had a strange pull. His people were on It and brought in others that gave him a report on it's material and the tracking device on it. They put the bug on a regular subliminal bible and watched who came to get it and losing a carrier who was dying of cancer as the enemy shot at him. He was told it was dark, waiting to be released and would wreak havoc if they slipped on the covers they manufactured. Through trade off they learned where it was from by the end of the day and who was releasing and targeting it to the other races. He immediately set about a press release to speak about the deception and how to recognize it, then also to release the other three subliminals in a huge big advertising, marketing campaign. He could tell that a number of his people that had worked on the first subliminal had gone over or had some contact with the other side. The bugs and trackers inside each evil book could be defeated by a satellite signal and since it worked on and amplifier system embedded in the book, they could shut off the spiritual power it radiated and cause the books to spontaneously burn all by themselves if given the correct code. He turned it over to satellite people pumping the subliminal bible over the global television and airwaves and had it communicate its' satellite programming would be down across the world. He then gave them the effective code he received from one of the people who was deep inside the darkness and had it beam from the same communication killer satellite in the orbit of other killer satellites in a mock war game. Across the world ignitions where causing explosions, spontaneous fires and incendiary incidents as it wreaked havoc across the planet and forces tried to stop the satellite but it's position and the firing on it would spark a huge satellite destruction war and halt business movement across the earth. So the satellite continued its' quick orbit across the planet burning up more storage, printing and postal businesses until the books were declared unlawful. He slept well that night until he woke with a start.

It was something he had to do and dialing a special number in the cellphone he was signaling his people to enact both company satellites. There was enemy around as he heard a car squeal off driving fast in the distance. The gravity mining, he immediately began rerouting and to pay the billion to NASA to scuttle their project and put his most advanced satellite into orbit. He sweated until it got done, and the finances became available. His people where paying a heavy cost to find out information about the enemy and where the dark books where headed to which was mostly subversive groups and a huge internet launch. The launch of the other free Subliminal bibles signaled the enemy as their operations sped up. They had several of their chief members that defected and where invaluable sources of knowledge as they messed up their most valuable areas by hacking and subversive work. The satellite in space came just in tim, as its' launch and codes began to cause ignition of the books in storage. The press themselves did the digging speaking of it being a deceptive copy and he commented that it must be terrorists and had spread across the globe. That had world resources capturing and destroying centers and capturing the people in production effectively causing the evil workers and the work to dissolve. The top forty members of the enemy design team where captured and reprogrammed to the truth for 3 months. Only when they were truly born again were they released. The killer satellite he was using was taken out and he barely got the newer satellite up in time for the subliminal transmissions to earth.

The government, then threaten to halt the printing of all subliminal bibles and media/internet communication because of the "internal combustion" of the false bibles. He was prepared to go to code "red" as he saw other elements beginning to rally behind the edict as he advanced many lawyers into the fray and political help. The UN joined in the attack after two months and he knew something sinister was behind it. Code red went to dark red as he went to underground publishing facilities and went on the alert as his gravity mining ships where being tracked and laws were being enacted from them selling in some countries and he had to go black market. He halted the lawyers as he needed a trillion for Israel and saw the world leaders legislate the buying or selling of the subliminal bibles illegal. It was another month before the news articles and magazine reporters spoke about the gravity miners at length looking at documented evidence of a new technology. He made sure that the gravity technology could be scrapped, disposed of and disassembled in a time fashionably before being dropped in the sea before their assailants boarded. He also began pushing distribution of the malaria cure, diabetes cure and the substitute chocolate material that could stabilize low and high blood pressure with a stable diet. This caught the public by surprised as he published the cures in full page ads and his stocks began to soar immediately. There were some elements in the global governments that did not like the cures and immediately had the gravity carriers halt and decease their activities and return to various countries to be boarded. They were mostly in Russia hitting vast diamond storage on the ocean floor and a rare type of crystal that had unique transmission qualities. They were allowed to finish their sales on the black market before being confiscated and under a new law being called seized by countries. The lost affected him greatly as did the knowledge of the profit from the cures and the last gravity mining would be drained in a few months in the rising African monetary, stock and trade economy. The continent still needed an influx of billions in finances until the end of the year to hold them over in the world's recession. To further complicate things, word came that at the last concert tour of the season in Australia that Kalani "kneed" a man between his legs after he slipped on stage and during a turn grabbed her, kissed her and squeezed her hip. She promptly left the stage outraged and then later felt remorse and asked about the young gentlemen in custody and decided not to press charges and wanted to see him. She apologized to him, taught him how he should engage a woman. He was young, a nerd and infatuated. Her time with him proved effective as when he left a bevy of women where there to ask him if he was really with Kalani. Her security reported he looked like he was in good hands as he drove off with one of them. It hit the press that night and the next day and he told her not to worry about it, it would blow over and she could make amends at a Jewish concert in Israel in two weeks. He actually needed the time with Kalani and her worry to calm him as they mostly slept together for days. Their problems seem to melt away as she spoke it wasn't correct what she had done and met with him to be shone around Israel and photo ops of them walking by the sea, laughing, and her walking with his sisters. It was during that time she felt she needed to tone down the sensual nature of her dancing and identity and draw closer to God in pure worship. They accepted her there and asked why she believed in Yahshua the Messiah and her clear answers being Spirit led captured their hearts as the families around her came to Yahshua. The concert was a success and someone had her quickly ushered from the country before others heard first hand of her love for Yahshua. She found a way to worship from a pure heart on guitar and piano and wanted to change the concert

DANIEL E. SPRINGS

style and material for her next album. She was telling him all about it as she came home jet-lagged as he worried about the African financial market. Something told him not to as he remembered the words of Yahshua the messiah, "Why do you worry?" then he gave it back to God asking where is your answer. He wanted to get up but Kalani made a sound not to move. At breakfast she was happy. I need to drive he told her, just to get away to get some idea, up to NY. Call me when you get back? She said and asked. Thank you he told her. I need to work on the album she said and told him to take the 911 turbo boosted up with better tires, a nitrous system, an extra compressed gas tanks-she said to get him back quicker. She was at the door, hair down looking sexy after a kiss watching him leave as she prayed to God around his neck to keep her husband safe. He didn't know why but stopped twice for gas and to just walk before continuing. Then just inside the city something told him to be at a certain spot quickly and he pushed it. When he got to the spot he saw a woman running around a corner being fired at by two men and he drove to her telling the well-dressed woman to get in. She didn't hesitate and he was moving before she closed the door. At an intersection bullets rained from an SUV at the bullet proof glass as it took a curve to catch them. The steering and taking curves allowed him to get ahead of their attackers as the guns kept firing. At the interstate he hit the nitrous as a helicopter was coming into view. He lost them out of their sight and taking several curves through a tree lined residential district as the sun was setting and called a number and cruised up to a residence with the garage door opening and closing. Valerie the beautiful German dame identified him by her IPOD camera, and fingerprint her advanced system scanned off button he touched on the dash. She asked about the residence he said was off the grid in another name and waited inside as they listened for and watched the helicopter moving in patterns seeking them but unable to "sight them" move away. She then told him her family was trying to kill her, breaking down in tears as he held her. A family that was heavy in the weapons dealing since WW2 had amassed a 12 trillion dollar family fortune and a reputation as one of the top weapon dealers in the world. It had caused infighting and attack of enemies and half their family was dead as her side was being wiped out because of their elder inheriting and the lot had fallen to her as the eldest daughter. She wanted no part of it but it had been thrust on her and so far she had avoided food poisoning, three assassination attempts and a car bomb. He got her a beer and started dinner of lamb as she asked about Kalani and then the gossip about the gravity carriers, if the gravity device was real and if he really was behind the African continent' rise to prominence. He had been talked about and in she had heard gossip about him and the need to make him pay. She added to the lamb and made the salad while he worked on an appetizer and more vegetables and showed her from a device the gravity carriers. She calculated the material gross of various valuable resources he had extracted and put into the African market staggering at the thought as her knife rested near her salad plate. He concurred with her assessment and eyes narrowing with insight she spoke that was why they took his company and how it would leave the African continent defenseless in the coming collapse and economic attacks. She had seen and heard the plans at the L4 conferences that spoke of the world economic plans leading up to the coming of the Christ. He had gotten in the way a little but for the most part his work could not alter the long range goals set by those in high seats and places of power. He corrected her by saying it was God's work, he then watched as the lamb was consumed and she gave him a website to look at that showed the whole outlay, there for people to see but no one ever looked on the internet. She told him L4 was more disturbed about his (the Lord's) bibles believing it was bringing to many to Christ and the plans made to halt if it hadn't work, so there where people following it's every move to destroy it. He spoke about the DNA and asked who they had planted in his organization as he also spoke of its dispensing to other ethnic societies. She said a records keeper and that he had better get finished before the onslaught took place. She used a code to get into the L4 mainframe showing him all the info they had on his secret publishing facilities and new plans for Africa's implosion and demise. She surmised he would need trillions heavily invested in profitable world markets over time to keep the African continent' financial market growing and safe. The L4's global market plan was "the plan" for the next few years and she showed the outlay and where they should invest. Then she made an agreement to give ten trillion for under-girding The African economy through investment in the world markets. She had to find her banker (which was the reason she left Germany) to do the transaction of funds and he set it up with his people. His people would invite the banker to a business luncheon with his favorite entrees and "beverages" in a closed sealed room and then present her to the banker. It was transferred the next day at eleven am after the banker was surprised to see her and being threaten to lose all the families business if he did not. They celebrated and she received messages that her family wanted to talk, would stop the murdering, and be given the rightful headship. They needed the last two trillion immediately as she had exposed their flank and their enemies where already attacking mercilessly and they were losing their status in the L4 and in the hierarchy of the German community. She stayed that afternoon as she talked about how the global world leader would come to power, all that was planned, military things she didn't understand but could see the stolen knowledge of the gravity carriers would play a great part. She overlapped it with Revelations, and said she once believed but was now a little lamb that had lost its' way in the forest of the deceitfulness of riches. She saw the wolf coming but was laying there under plush covers and didn't want to come out and had felt the wolf's hot breath. He spoke about the good shepherd coming after her, wooing her, picking her up if she wanted to come. This broke Valerie's heart and at a moment of indecision he said "let's pray." Tears broke her eyes as she started slowly crying out to Jesus, then saying she wanted to come back home, was so sorry and then slip to her knees, begging Jesus, confessing her sins, asking forgiveness and when she allowed Christ to have the supremacy and primary place in her heart, she felt the joy of the Lord. She smiled as she left with his people into a stealth plane to be taken back to Germany. He flew home to a happy wife saying someone had underwritten her new concert format and incredibly her people wanted her in two months for a world tour as the market was hungry and ready. She told him she had to pray and fast for God's leading wondering if no sex was okay for a week getting his consent. He understood saying he hoped it didn't begin that night. She said "no silly." he had to go to Africa anyway taking a flight out in the morning and returned at the end of the week to full plans and the concert setup done. When he returned and he had to make distribution decisions for the new bible and watch the steady stream of data that the other societies where advancing at an accelerated pace with the new subliminal bibles. His mind was focused on helping the young people understand decision making and to be inspired to achieve. He had no ideas come to him or his people accept the generic ones and decided to wait over the weekend as Kalani received the vision and she was moving on it, worshiping, recording and making preparations for another world tour to start. Saturday she was having another big meeting as everything was moved up to three weeks. He kissed her quick then went to a gym to play some ball and after stopped at a fast food place and sat with his lunch while some cheerleaders had his car boxed in. a football coach introduced himself and as they sat they began talking. The football coach told him how he was able to inspire kids. He taught them it was not so much about winning but helping them to mature as men. Success he said meaning more so how to use their abilities when the exact time was right. He spoke of things his coach taught him and the way he inspired kids even cutting sitting out a top female on the basketball team until she learned the team wasn't about her. The coach also related a young man that was a great singer, had a great family and sports ability but swore and cussed which wasn't allowed. He was not allowed to play and transferred but found trouble also with his next team. The discipline and ability to build them gave him the greatest joy. He talked to a coach about a book inspiring young people with the wisdom, discipline, encouragement and understanding of what life was really about and what was expected of every young person. They formulated a system to talk to a thousand other coaches and collate their thoughts, wisdom and anecdotes and then DVD's with it to put them right in the middle of one on one Coach/athlete talks, in the locker room, and the office of coaches and how they handled troubled players. A key story he gave was on a young man that wanted to quit the football team and a coach telling him if he quit the team it would start a progression of him quitting other things in life. The young people needed to be "fired up!" He talked to a series of coaches and got the project off the ground as Kalani agreed with it and then told him they wanted to start the world tour now. He wasn't ready for it but impossibly they already had stadiums and gigs lined up and sold out concerts as soon as they announced it. Something was happening and she said she felt the time was now God was calling her. Okay was all he could say as she made calls, and went into deeper prayer. It was needful as she was a totally different creature on stage worshiping and praising God with her whole being drawing the crowds into total worship and watching the cities waiting for God to move in them.

He was called back to Africa to help with the economy of the continent and to finish a book and web media presence with encouragement and teaching biblical lessons and responsibility to young people. At the end of the year she was finishing another CD ready to start another world tour as the public wanted more of the God who led her. The anointing fell in concerts and on her CD listeners who got blessed when her voice went up several octaves by the spirit. The next year it was said angels could be heard in the concerts and her fourth world tour it was said she glowed while on stage. Five years he steadily worked with the economy of Africa, as it grew to self-sustaining and people took care of the mass media project going global using the encouragement through sports. He rarely saw Kalani except when they were scheduled to meet and at a few promotions. Kalani was gone in the Spirit, she glowed spending time with the Lord in so much it translated bringing all near her up into another level of Christ. She was worn out after five years but kept saying there was more to do, he understood the feeling as world economies where now catching up to Africa and the monetary unit becoming weaker as societies with the subliminal bibles where sparked to increase with the new technical knowledge that increase all GNP's. It was a delicate situation as he had to keep world balance away from measures by the elitist controlling the world to throw it in disarray. The US was still floating with a huge debt at times finding him in the way as he approached countries with better plans for agriculture, mineral use etc. and used Kalani's staggering income to broker deals. He waited for her on an island when they both needed a rest and he found just before the plane landed she had passed away of exhaustion and he held her lifeless body for hours rocking her. The press went on to say he was a cruel taskmaster and pushed her to broker world deals and support Africa as the world spoke she was someone they would miss. The pressure was tremendous and he stayed on the island only until the day of the funeral then he returned. Her finances kept him helping with economies as he sold their homes and everything to hungry greedy fans that wanted a piece of her at no expense even desiring a museum for her. Sitting by the sea one day after hearing someone had desecrated her burial site to sale her cadaver on the internet being foiled by an inner satellite alarm after disabling all others. A call came from a secretary in the US telling him that America was in serious trouble with many nations over the debt and there was a close session of nations that spoke of a time to bring them to the table, the Nation needed his help, he simply asked what could he do and weighed it in with all else going on. Finally after walking by the sea in tears telling the Lord he couldn't handle it, he sat by a rock and fell asleep sending an email out on his net-book to do what they wanted in the Kalani situation. He woke in a vision to America in red white and blue garb looking at him, telling him to get up and look at the sea. She spoke the sea had so much power if it could be generated. Two children were playing on the beach building a sand castle with a plastic model on top of it. He went over to ask what it was and they told him it was a sea generator silly, it gave electricity. Then they gave him measurements as he put it in his net-books, specifics of how it operated, even backwards and taking him down to the sea they showed him how much water he needed, and where it should be placed, solar fusion to get it started, composite material that would not rust or erode by the salt and how to make the material. As sun was setting he had to help them finish the sand castle before darkness came. When he asked who was their daddy, they giggled finishing then ran away waving by. When he woke his secretary was ascending in a helicopter on the beach telling him he must come to NY for the Kalani situation then to Washington. He look to see the net book had the wave generator sea design and he saved people as he called top engineers and ocean scientists for an emergency meeting in NY. He made a statement about Kalani's contribution, the glory of God in her life before visiting the desecrated area as the global film crews and reporters watched. He simply sat crossing his fingers in sadness as others came over until pieces where hauled away and new pieces brought in. He stayed the next few days until her burial site was totally restored with a more protective triple threat security system. Washington was calling every day and his engineers and ocean people met with him every day as he took the design to global proportions wondering where it would be most feasible, how long down coast lines, how long to set up plants, how cheaply the composites could be made. The last day he ignited a flame of her memory. May what God gave her to do be always remembered . . . and may her memory evoke us to serve God, giving Him the highest honor, glory and praise. He was taken to Washington that night after America's view changed of him, to someone who really loved Kalani-his wife. The White House was in a fit and he was asked immediately what all the plans where for and global beach territories as the door was closed to a crowded Oval Office needing answers as his computer and drafts where all ready scanned and copies given by the time he left entrance security. He asked how bad the world situation was then talked about what if he could save countries 70% of fuel generations. He spoke about The Lord giving him a vision then mentioned the design concepts. There was real time connection with everyone on his team and the efficiency of computer and test models. Then he spoke the cost to nations what would they pay for it, wiping out US debts, and giving them the chance to install their own or the US installing and controlling how many for environmental and safety sake. They were interested in the solar fusion reactor which he held out to assurances of patent rights, trained workers, a discourse with world leaders, limited use on the solar technology and use for guns, missiles and weapons, etc. the president asked at the end what he personally wanted out of all this then commented that the beach house rental would soon be up and spoke of some property the government had taken away. He had cleared the Oval officer at various parts of the discussion and finally alone with him wanted to discuss the African economic question. The trade imbalance was causing a 2 to 1 monetary deficit and he opened a folder of how to get America back to prosperity sharing in business production, solar fusion to jump start factories and sell electricity overseas, etc. Then he went in specifics of turning the country back to God which the President said he would think about being non-com-mental and ending the night expressing sorrow for his wife, the incident and if there was anything he could do.

A car picked him up and he was taken to a large ultramodern Virginia house with several levels on a wide track of land with many servants. His team met in a top secret facility in DC as the project was announced and given to world economies that lapped at the thought of it and finding it theoretically sound. Trillions disappeared from the debt in the next month as countries moved swiftly to implement the technology except in America where public utilities fought it tooth and nail as the first several generators where implemented. It was a losing battle but the President gave them a year to reconstruct their utilities. It was a waste he thought as he particularly worked with the generators on the African coast and disadvantaged third world countries that would need outside monetary resources to help implement the technology. He was a leader speaking to the rich rather quickly as everyone got on board with the new technology and didn't want to see any disparity and came away feeling wonderful after being told what it could do for the nations. It was at one of these charity dinners he was pushing before impostors, con men and other charities latched on to the idea for profiting and money making schemes that he met an emissary sent by a secretary in one of the offices. She discussed a one million dollar gift asking specifics as they got on an elevator, there she held it asking if he thought he was pretty smart getting the National Debt erased and this new technology to all the countries for international peace? She then laid it out for him as they descended another floor and she stopped it again. She spoke the President had people working on EM, Solar Fusion and Wave generator technology for military defense purposes. The nations where still going to make the US pay but for bringing him to the mat, the President was going to make them pay in an all-out war that would decimate and divide the planet up like a Risk or Monopoly game leaving untold decimated. On the 1st floor she ask should they have lunch by a fountain and used a scrambler as she did in the elevator to impede listening to their conversation. She allowed him to hear White House conversations about preparations, the next election etc. She spoke he just gave him the credit card for more military, satellite and orbit technology to decimate the planet. Thank you. However . . . she coaxed him there maybe is a way to put a lid on the technology and stop what was being planned. Someone powerful had to run against him in the next election and who better than a Nobel Prize winner. I hardly, he spoke before she cut him off. His attributes, accomplishments, tragedy's etc., made for a candidate with a strong public persona and women loved him. When his record came to light about how he helped the continent and brokered deals on a global scale plus a bible and conservative glean that had helped many and charity giving . . . well. This is not too late, she spoke already in the process stage, everything must come out, before it's distorted in the press which you have in your back pocket as the underdog. Look I . . . yes or no? The technologies are out there and about to use. After he said yes she smiled and told him to give the government back their houses and a suitable place would be found in his home state. He asked her if she was always this persuasive and if she got what she wanted? Yes she said without hesitation, smiling and leaving politely for any cameras, as he did also, getting up to leave also as the chauffeur tried to butter him up and ask about the conversation. They were all spies he said telling him about an etiquette error of one of his team in the White House. He went to a park to get away that night and a runner came up to drink from the fountain near him telling him about a old mill house in North Carolina and a motorcycle behind a building, a gym to change his clothes and scrub hard, bugs where everywhere. He was also to clear out a government account in his name of 100 million and switch it into a portfolio with his clothes. She sauntered off as he obeyed instructions and arrived at the mill house with the wheel still functioning, peaceful and serene and a high tech interior with four floors. Behind in the barn a staff already had his projections, campaign and schedule in full swing stopping to cheer as he was led into the web center, finance, film-studio, speech-writing, and conference room where they were discussing every part of his political landscape and asking about who he would like as a wife from a stack of portfolios and a short list. His campaign adviser said they could wait it was probably too soon as one pointed out a female who was a great catch about to get away. He said he would take a look at them. In the reporter media room he was sat down for questioning and to see how he would answer political questions, plus others getting an idea of his rhythm. The Nobel candidates came out the next week with his name on it, he was taught political science, the name of every player in DC government and world politics as a Grass-Roots foundation began on that swell to politely discuss his name for the presidency. With tinkering it

continued until a full groundswell and notice by the press who were able
to corner him at a beautiful Wilmington University and nice backdrop for
his announcement. However, the day before he had told them he had never
asked god which put a halt on everything. Then taking his time he did and
then said if he will allow me, so be it. Then taking his time picking his
battles as the press kits told about his inspiration for the design of the wave
generators etc., he built steam slowly and confidently working with young
people and after accepting the Nobel letting the media attention drive the
campaign into second gear. There were questions arising about his mate,
as they were fended off by his wife just dying and how to get the American
Economy working and providing decent hospital and insurance coverage
without socializing. He had to meet people he despised to carry favor and
waiting on what God told him to say, often shocking them and asking
about their eternal salvation before a presentation of the gospel.

They noted him as someone who stood for his convictions. He followed
his play-makers and won debates candidly, speaking soundly to the press,
inspiring confidence. He was the front runner in his party after another
year as he pulled away from the pack putting together a software package
for teachers to use across the nation and providing finances from the
software company to finance teacher salaries and school building. His
people bugged him about the list for marital candidates but none struck
him as e was looking for something more Christ like in the character. He
did however meet an interesting female one night after a fundraiser in a
science museum as he relaxed after-wards and discussing his campaign with
several upper-crust families he was led away after-wards to the basement as
they discussed matters with a curator then the administration head as he
was told about the coming attraction and given a glimpse. It was quiet
boring and they left after a while for dinner unable to get another seat in
the museum restaurant for him. He insisted they please go ahead as he had
to make calls and would catch them at the bar after-wards. Taking calls and
answering emails he set on a marble bench until he finished them and
closed his eyes for a moment. Waking by a water fall nearby he went into a
section where an African-American female was working on a section of a
dinosaur fossil. She didn't recognize him, immediately telling him about
her work before asked. She explained things on a more evolutionist bent
which caused him to smile at parts and chuckle expressing doubts at several
of her theories, citing creation scientist sources that immediately left her
scrambling for more support asking if he was a Creationist. He affirmed

her belief and left her doubting with other sources as he attacked her geological time-line, the prevalent big-bang theory without God and inaccuracies in Darwinian thought. She stopped her work going to books and also on the internet to correct his interpretations but found them to be sound as he directed her to go to more viable resources on the internet. She called them biased and after a while objected to scouring for more and she began attacking the bible as he put up a ready defense of Genesis and the Old Testament with scientific proof that rocked her foundation. She simply said it was inconclusive and began to go back to work saying it was full of myths as he did spoke to her about the Christ and evidence of his resurrection. She then said she didn't want to hear anymore just before his PA came up and told him they had left upstairs and another meeting that he could attend. His PA gave her his card after he said he looked forward to talking to her again. Glancing at the card she listened as his PA told her he had an opening for a lunch in another city and she immediately said she couldn't make it before telling her to send her a first class airline ticket, hotel reservation and limo before saying thank you and ushering her out. He was surprised to see her at lunch after he had been in the dining room all day schmoozing political movers he would need in his campaign. She looked lovely and delved right in to inaccuracies of his faith of which he corrected her showing her scripture in the bible of which after a while she asked him not to use it. She went back to scientific evidence of which he gave her a list of Creationist sources and equivocal proof that she finally ask him to put away the computer. She became more insistent as dessert was brought saying he can't throw away today's science and spoke about the dark ages as he countered telling her what Paul the Apostle said about not arguing about science, the 51 theses that brought the world out of the dark ages, and noted Christian scientists from the 1200's until today and how they saw things and through their work glorified God more and saw more of the glory of God. She couldn't believe some of the people he mentioned, then said she had to leave as she stopped his hand from going to the net-book. She said she enjoyed the lunch and thanked him leaving in a confident, controlled anger fashion knowing he was watching her. She held in a breath as a waiter impeded her progress of leaving more quickly. He spoke he hoped they could do it again over dinner. They had a series of calls more arguing and finally she invited him to her home for a nice dinner. She had a PHD with her springing her trap as they began cordially discussing over dinner until the physicists began speaking his specialty and he countered with other physicists noted with the Creationist views. Miriam got mad with him then feeling he was insulting the professor with a doctorate joining his side then deescalating the discussion with dessert and another tact attacking the Hebrew and Greek of the Old and New Testament. He was more than ready with a history of the bible, various Codex's and proof what was said in Hebrew before we have today. The professor left as he spoke of the crux of Isaiah 53 about the Messiah and the universe not being able to exist or create by itself needing a powerful god to create, order and sustain it using quotes from scientist. They are not scientist he yelled. He simply then ask him what was the definition of a scientists and did it fit them. Rubbish he said leaving. Miriam then in anger after he left asked why he had to be correct all the time? Then followed up with if part of the world became Christian it just couldn't survive. Why not he asked? She told him to please leave then. He did going out into the December night seeing a female talking to Jesus further up the street, with tears asking God why? She went to a park and unburdened her heart ask why in her life, the rape, incest, drug abuse, just about everything a person can handle. She was about to say she didn't want it anymore, "I know I'm supposed to go to Washington." She then stated that she had car payments, school loans, and the landlord and telling him she just wanted to get away to an island in the pacific and have coffee with a nice MC-Donald's breakfast. She said she was tired and then receiving an answer said yes Lord. And spoke about the abuse ministry she worked at and children ministry needing a van. He heard her again say okay and began to leave and followed her to her apartment, up several flights of stairs and to the place where a door shut and began to make phone calls. She woke up to hear her college loans had been paid and her rent was paid up and watched her cry as she saw a big MC-Donald's bag at her door saying thank you Jesus. She cried again she saw a sign saying her car had been repossessed and in its' place was a new Chrysler van and Escalade for her. Her friend from the center came down to cry with her and take the van. She got a call in the car about a vacation package at a spa with airline tickets free but she had to leave her job and take the spa package, she said she would call them back. He called her then and told her to do it that he would need a person with her political background on his campaign committee. He didn't let her ask any questions saying all would be provided, a place for her to stay in DC and a bank account solely in her name in case she decided to leave. Then he said he would see her in DC and sent a psychologist to befriend her and help her through certain issues. When the psychologist called and said she was looking extremely beautiful after spa treatments and an excellent workout routine desiring to go out dating he took a week off in the islands. He took her to excellent places every night for dinner sending her a different expensive gown that excelled her beautiful. Nights of love she dreamed of the night she would never have to let him go. It was the sixth night a Saturday that he took her to a pleasant dinner with her in a green gown that he proposed to her. He flew two of her girlfriends' and an older gentleman that she knew to give her away and in a white gown surprised her bringing her up to a second floor balcony overlooking the sea. A minister was there as he brought her to their extravagant picture perfect wedding with white columns and flowers music and photography. He took her to another place for their wedding chamber with a huge bath for their love. He entwined his fingers in hers desiring a child, she was more than happy to fulfill his request. When they returned to DC after another week vacation his staff began speaking to her about the duties of the First lady and how to handle political questions. Her "with child" state caused her not to be in the debates with the President's wife. This saved him time and caused the nation to wonder about her ability in the role of first lady. This was until they agreed to a debate after the media caught their opponents' wife in a blunder. The nation was surprised at her knowledge of issues, easy speaking, joking and being on the defensive with adept answers that easily deflected all arguments. It cemented his win as it pulled him ahead in the polls. When she was attacked later on her medical record and her family's dysfunction they spoke about her being in charge of looking at the mental health system in America and doing something about it. This again swayed the public toward her idealism and got them into office. It was at dinner on the voting night as the nation looked on that she was in a beautiful gown having a lovely dinner, signaling they were unafraid of the results as the public looked on as they went to four different places. She voted for her husband had an effect as other women saw her beauty and opinion and followed suit. The first night in office her gown again carried the country's favor as he began halting the use of EM, Solar Fusion, etc., for military weapons use. She came in to his office with her gown when he told her just a little while longer and set on his desk sensually. He put up the paperwork up after signing an executive order for subliminal bibles to be legal again. The American economy was still in a mess incurring more debt and its' enemies more active. He returned prayer to schools, the Ten-Commandments to state and federal buildings and outlawed abortions. He took homosexuality out of the schools, military, media and public arena and made sodomy a public offense. He was heavy handed but it steered America back to God as answers came for its' economic growth, decrease in crime terrorism and natural disasters and women and men returning to excellent health with the aged being cared for. The wisdom in science, technology and mathematics put them far ahead again in technological expertise and productivity increased in the country. The number of children four kept his popularity from slipping as each time her glowing face graced covers of magazines. Creationism and the bible taught in school and evolution being outdated really caused a public cry-out and his wife's attention to the elderly, under mental care, that took a lot of State's budgets as they were constrained to help their citizens. Mining saved the economy as they did it quicker and faster and added elements to metals that made them stronger and the most desired and expensive on the market. The anti-malaria medicine found, calming perfume and a chocolate that restored metabolism ending diabetes, lowering cholesterol and high blood where the top exports as was a liquid that made fabric fibers stronger. With these and many other products given by wisdom from the Lord America came back to prominence living 77% on wave generators 16% on solar power and 5% on wind generation to fuel the whole country and prayer. Others were taking the credit for it at election time as he was working on keeping the world economies up and balanced praying to the Lord continually with a massive prayer effort and bringing the full light of the gospel to each nation continuously with many missionaries that the nation funded. Special blue-diamonds found mostly in America was fueling it's come back as everyone bartered for these rare and exceptional stones that where hungered by technology markets. Fertilizers that where enriched with bio-nutrients was the biggest export converting huge tracts of infertile soils into plush farmlands across the world. Three times a day he as President had people pray to the Lord God of heaven and instituted a fasting and praying program with special days of citizens in sackcloth. This his adversaries and detractors hated most and wanted to leave the Presidency and crying out to voters against him especially young voters and a groundswell of the wealthy in ungodliness and suburbanites who wanted their own will and live as their own gods in their private serfdom. America's weight and health they especially pushed citing citizens weren't losing weight fast enough although he had instituted polices of exercise periods in schools, gyms and playgrounds every few miles and caused fat losses of 20% across the board by innovative media advertisement and incentives. The governor of Texas really ragged on his case about the issue making it paramount before the election speaking what he would do to have a cleaner, leaner, meaner America pushing himself ahead in the polls and daring him to come to Texas for a face-off where he was not loved. On a major challenge as the governor gathered other governors in a 5k run to show solidarity and challenge the President to get healthy and come down if he wasn't afraid and join us, showing America he cared. The President chose to remain silent working on other issues and strengthening the economy by God's help while pushing 3 million in a little known triathlon at the last minute to make it comfortable for his Spartan wife after pregnancy and two secret service people to participate and push her to win. It was a triathlon that many people missed and looked over because of its' small standard and lack of organization and great prizes. She was relatively unknown or cared about as not being in the Texas or triathlete communities. The only stipulation as donors they made was no one else could sign up after a certain date and it wasn't pumped in the media. People where surprised how luxurious it was on race day. The President's wife got all the advantageous having the best equipment, knowing about the course and being put out front with her security that looked like just other female runners. Volunteers where paid which gave them extra incentive to help the runners and she had special volunteers that helped her at the change phases in the race in special ways. Cameras where limited except for special media cameras for her editing her run in the best light and following her. When the governor finished the 5k with his cohorts he directly challenged the President calling him a coward for not showing support and getting support from other political pundits in the news until his aid was asked after-wards about what he felt about the insult to the President. Then his press secretary spoke about hours ago his wife the first lady winning a triathlon in the state of Texas that day and giving the half million dollar purse to support several needed gyms and exercise facilities across the state by God's help. It threw egg on the face of the governor and his cohorts as the secretary said they would need to step up their physical fitness policy and taught them more about the better, more attractive president's initiative. It changed the election as he held and rubbed his wife that night, she actually enjoyed it and seeing the clips of the event the next two weeks as it showed how it knocked out and torpedoed the governor's run against him for the party's nomination. It also made others wary and intimidated as his wife set a bar that many could not reach and declared them well ahead of other nominees in agility and fitness. His political machine worked with this to show how well he did and excelled in other areas and kept steamrolling from that point on. It kicked off a national fitness craze his wife had to push as she was desired at running events everywhere and entered in at other Iron man competitions. That pushed them in the electoral race and a win as she won a marathon the day before the election as they showed the cushy camp of his competitor and his travels and politicking on the last day whereas he spent time after the marathon with his wife to recuperate telling the press he was giving her foot massages and clips of her running in the surprised marathon caught the envy of the nation again. It was said he ran away with the election the next day in the press, as her courage changed the thinking of a nation that anything could be possible to those that believed.

CPSIA information can be obtained at www.ICGtesting.com
Printed in the USA
BVOW082317090113

310209BV00002B/100/P